W9-BRS-993

CAPTURED

An American Prisoner of War in North Vietnam

CAPTURED

AN AMERICAN PRISONER OF WAR IN NORTH VIETNAM

BY ALVIN TOWNLEY

SCHOLASTIC
FOCUS
NEW YORK

Copyright © 2019 by Alvin Townley

All rights reserved. Published by Scholastic Focus, an imprint of Scholastic Inc., *Publishers since 1920.* SCHOLASTIC, SCHOLASTIC FOCUS, and associated logos are trademarks and/or registered trademarks of Scholastic Inc.

The publisher does not have any control over and does not assume any responsibility for author or third-party websites or their content.

Library of Congress Cataloging-in-Publication Data

Names: Townley, Alvin, author.
Title: Captured : an American prisoner of war in North Vietnam / by Alvin Townley.
Other titles: American prisoner of war in North Vietnam
Description: New York : Scholastic Focus, [2019] | Includes bibliographical references and index.
Identifiers: LCCN 2018016709 | ISBN 9781338255669
Subjects: LCSH: Denton, Jeremiah A., Jr. (Jeremiah Andrew), 1924-2014—Juvenile literature. | Vietnam War, 1961-1975—Prisoners and prisons, North Vietnamese—Juvenile literature. | Prisoners of war—United States—Juvenile literature. | Prisoners of war—Vietnam—Juvenile literature. | Vietnam War, 1961-1975—Personal narratives, American—Juvenile literature.
Classification: LCC DS559.4 .T686 2019 | DDC 959.704/3092--dc23 LC record available at https://lccn.loc.gov/2018016709

10 9 8 7 6 5 4 3 2 1   19 20 21 22 23

Printed in the U.S.A.   23

First edition, April 2019

Book design by Becky James

To the American POWs
who returned with honor
and to the families
who never forgot

CONTENTS

Introduction		xi
Chapter 1	Capture	1
Chapter 2	Hỏa Lò Prison	11
Chapter 3	The Zoo	35
Chapter 4	Pigeye	64
Chapter 5	The Interview	73
Chapter 6	Parade	83
Chapter 7	Back to the Zoo	97
Chapter 8	Little Vegas	109
Chapter 9	Alcatraz	126
Chapter 10	1968	144
Chapter 11	Change	158
Chapter 12	Camp Unity	178
Chapter 13	Homecoming	193
Epilogue		207
Bibliography		213
Endnotes		219
Photograph and Map Credits		225
Index		227
Acknowledgments		237
About the Author		239

INVICTUS

Out of the night that covers me,
Black as the pit from pole to pole,
I thank whatever gods may be
For my unconquerable soul.

In the fell clutch of circumstance
I have not winced nor cried aloud.
Under the bludgeonings of chance
My head is bloody, but unbowed.

Beyond this place of wrath and tears
Looms but the Horror of the shade,
And yet the menace of the years
Finds and shall find me unafraid.

It matters not how strait the gate,
How charged with punishments the scroll,
I am the master of my fate,
I am the captain of my soul.

"INVICTUS" BY WILLIAM ERNEST HENLEY
A POEM PASSED AMONG AMERICAN PRISONERS OF WAR
IN NORTH VIETNAM (1965-1973).

INTRODUCTION

ON BRIGHT MORNINGS, Jerry watched the sunlight trace a path across his floor. Its transit always proved brief, lasting just the fleeting moments rays could angle through the iron bars of his cell's lone window. When the patch of light disappeared, he turned to the cockroaches, ants, and occasional rats that scurried across his floor; their movements brought his static world rare variety. He silently observed mosquitoes alight on the sill, on the walls, and on his arms. Sometimes, he found energy to swat them away. Other times, he'd passively watch them suck their fill. If he squashed their bloated bodies, his own blood would splatter across his arm, leg, or whatever body part the mosquito had chosen for its meal. Blood would mingle with perspiration. He'd wipe up the mess with a dirty sleeve.

The temperature rose as the sun crossed the sky and stoked the Southeast Asian humidity. The hot air inside the walls hardly ever stirred; it was so thick he sometimes had trouble inhaling. He sipped his ration of water frugally, knowing the cup had to last most of the day. The ration never could replace what he sweated out, but he somehow managed. He moved as little as possible. He spent most days lying on a mat atop a raised concrete sleeping platform. The leg stocks at the platform's end reminded him of the punishment that typically accompanied upholding his sacred Code and refusing to submit to his captors' will. His ankles had spent time in the stocks before. When a man's honor is all he has left, he does not surrender it easily.

Jerry could only control what he said or wrote. The prison's cadre of guards and officers, the Camp Authority, governed everything else. His existence did not seem his own. Only the Camp Authority determined who and what passed through the padlocked door into his little room. They brought the greasy soup he had to eat. They brought him scraps of toilet paper; they dictated when he could bathe or empty his stinking latrine bucket. Worst, they opened the peephole at will, spying on him as if he were a lion in a zoo—an old grizzled lion, at that, he thought. And he knew their methods could best his willpower. If they wanted him to talk, to confess, they eventually succeeded. But never without a fight from their prisoner.

He owned nothing. The scant personal items in the room— the porcelain cup, ragged clothes, bamboo sleeping mat, and washcloth—were all issued. Guards called the scraps he collected in his cell, in the courtyard, and in the latrine contraband. A scavenged nail might become a prized possession until he'd lose it during an inevitable cell inspection. Yet, for those moments, harboring something forbidden gave him a soaring sense of victory.

Most moments just brought silence, melancholy, and an unchanging view of four drab concrete walls, a filthy concrete floor, and a plaster ceiling lit day and night by a dim bulb.

The sounds drifting over the big wall outside and through his window reminded him that life went on for everyone else. The soft chatter of merchants, the grunt of trucks shifting gears, the crunch of tires on dusty pavement all signaled the progression of life beyond his tiny, sequestered world. Life for Jerry drifted more toward simple existence than anything resembling the previous life he remembered. Although after interminable months locked away, he found himself doubting those memories. Was the life he recalled really his? What was real? What was just concocted by his desperate imagination?

The world he'd formerly known had, from his perspective, stopped spinning on July 18, 1965; he knew that much. Now, nearly one year later, he had little knowledge of that world. He couldn't trust the news passed along by the Camp Authority or the propaganda broadcasts piped into his cell. Yet he puzzled over what he did hear about the war and politics at home in the United States. He wondered if his family, friends, and shipmates even knew he was still alive. He'd begun to doubt he'd ever see them again.

A full year had passed since he last hugged his wife and seven children. He could still picture them in the front yard, framed by May flowers—he was sure it was May, May 1965—as he left for a deployment to the South China Sea. He'd promised he'd be home for Christmas. He sailed eastward aboard the aircraft carrier USS

Independence, transiting the Atlantic, Mediterranean, and Indian oceans to arrive off the coast of North Vietnam. Just one day before assuming command of his squadron, he'd lost his aircraft, been forced to eject, and wound up imprisoned in Hanoi, the enemy's capital. He spent Christmas alone, trying to picture his family opening presents without him. He hoped his youngest children would remember their father; he hoped his wife would wait for him.

To his family, he was becoming a memory. To the American military, he had become a prisoner of war. To the North Vietnamese, he was a war criminal. They constantly reminded him his trial was near; he would pay for crimes committed against innocents during an undeclared war. To himself, he remained an American naval officer, true to his Code. But he'd begun to wonder: Could his enemy strip that away too?

When evening came, he listened to the flop of sandals as guards left the grim corridors of cellblocks and went home, went to dinner, went somewhere of their choosing to live their lives. Perhaps they'd see their families, drink with friends, or simply read a book. Their leaving offered Jerry another reminder of these things denied him.

Rat-tat-a-tat-tat.

He heard the faint sound of knocking. His spirits lifted. He knew another American was nearby. With guards gone, they could communicate.

Rat-tat-a-tat-tat. It came again. It was the old five-beat "shave-and-a-haircut" jingle.

Jerry swung his wasted body to the floor and knelt near the wall. He placed one end of his drinking cup to his ear and the open end to the wall. He rapped his knuckles twice. Tat-tat—"two bits"—he tapped in reply. Two American prisoners of war had, in code, just reassured each other they were not alone, at least not tonight.

He learned Air Force ace Robbie Risner now occupied the adjacent cell. Thank God Risner knew him as Jerry, not *Jeremiah* as his captors called him. That small comforting knowledge restored a measure of humanity to his life; he was with a friend.

Jerry brought a dilemma to Risner. The commandant of the prison, a man the Americans called "Cat," had told Jerry that the next day, May 2, 1966, he would speak to a reporter. Cat demanded Jerry comply. He demanded Jerry parrot the North Vietnamese perspective. More torture would accompany any refusal, deviation, or especially any misbehavior on air. Jerry had been through the ropes—quite literally—enough to know the sincerity of the threat.

Via coded taps, he explained the situation to Risner. What should he do? Should he go? Should he cooperate? Should he continue to resist?

When Jerry joined the US Navy, he'd sworn an oath never to make disloyal statements, never to visit dishonor upon his fellow servicemen, never to say more than the minimum to any foreign captors. Yet he feared more torture would kill him. How could he abide by the Code and survive? How could he turn this circumstance to his advantage? He and Risner tapped back and forth. After a period of deep thought, Jerry tapped, "I'll go, and blow it wide open."

He and Risner offered a prayer together. Jerry signed off by tapping code for *G-B-U: God bless you*, a deeply meaningful term among the American prisoners of war. Then he lay down for his 288th night in North Vietnam's Hỏa Lò Prison. He fell asleep, confident in himself and his plan.

The next morning, a guard entered his cell and ordered him out. Jerry hated himself for the flicker of gratitude he felt as the guard released him from his confines. Anything beat the crushing monotony and loneliness of that infernal chamber—even the presence of an enemy. He left the cell and entered the courtyard. He quietly relished the open space around him. Then he focused on his mission. His shuffling steps gained purpose. The prisoner became a man once again.

Guards loaded their captive into an idling jeep. The gears engaged and Jerry Denton rolled toward a rendezvous with a foreign journalist who would unwittingly broadcast his secret message. The message Jerry sent would become one of the most ingenious and perhaps most desperate communications ever sent via television. He prayed someone in America would notice.

Chapter 1

CAPTURE

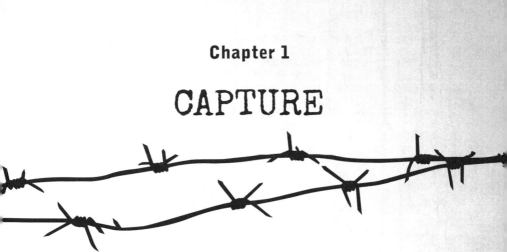

JERRY STOOD AT HIS SHIPBOARD desk and slipped off his US Naval Academy ring. "Class of 1947," it read. Nineteen years and two months had passed since the ceremony where he jubilantly tossed his hat into the air with his classmates and became a naval officer. Between his graduation and this day, Sunday, July 18, 1965, he had married his high school sweetheart and fathered seven children. In just two days, he would realize his dream of commanding an aircraft squadron at war.

He placed his ring in a drawer. Next to the ring, he placed his wedding band and a patch from his uniform. The patch read "CDR Jeremiah Denton" and bore the anchor and wings that marked him as a naval aviator. Commander Denton always removed these personal items before a mission. Doing so served as humble acknowledgment that a remote possibility of being shot down did, in fact, exist. No naval aviator, especially a veteran commander like Jerry, ever truly thought an enemy missile could catch him. On a ship, Jerry Denton was a good officer.

1

In the air, he was exceptional. Like most military aviators, he felt best in a cockpit. A thrill ran through him as he closed his cabin door and set out on the day's mission. He had no doubt that he would put his rings back on when he returned that afternoon.

Jerry's brown boots paced down narrow passageways of the aircraft carrier USS *Independence*. In the navy, only aviators wore brown boots; everyone else's were black. Jerry's distinctive boots were part of the trappings that built the spirit and ego of a naval aviator. These men were special.

The soft hum of machinery and hiss of ventilation helped him relax and focus on the mission ahead: another bombing run over North Vietnam. He walked the familiar route to the flight deck, climbed the usual ladders, and reached the last bulkhead. He opened the hatch.

Noise, fumes, sunshine, and heat immediately assailed him. Jerry shoved on his helmet and pulled down its dark visor. He still squinted against the brightness of midday in the South China Sea. The summer sun roasted steel, concrete, rubber, and men on the expansive four-acre flight deck, which felt conspicuously like a frying pan. Sunlight gleamed off the blue water, white aircraft, and glass canopies. His helmet provided little defense against the cacophony of jet noise. The moment a steam-driven catapult sent an aircraft howling off the bow, another aircraft would land near the ship's stern. It would ram its engines to full power in case its tailhook failed to snag one of four arresting cables strung across the deck. The air trembled with deafening noise.

Heavy exhaust made the humid air thicker still; air crew wore wet bandanas to help them breathe. Jerry felt sweat break out instantly; he noticed heat seeping through his boots. He hastened to his A-6 Intruder, nimbly weaving between taxiing aircraft, jet blasts, and whirling propellers; surviving on a flight deck was a vital art he'd had to master. Jerry knew one could be killed more easily on the deck than in the air.

Jerry arrived safely at his assigned aircraft from Attack Squadron 75, nicknamed the Sunday Punchers. He saw crewmen securing fourteen Mark 82 500-pound bombs to the Intruder's wings. To bear such a load, engineers had made the all-weather attack aircraft a big one. It weighed more than 60,000 pounds—30 tons. It stood sixteen feet tall. At six feet, Jerry's head barely reached the middle of the big plane's two distinctive gaping air intakes, which made the jet look like an oversized walrus missing its tusks.

Next to the plane, Jerry felt small. In the cockpit, he felt powerful. No average pilot could handle a beast as large and fast as an Intruder, fly it off a moving ship, then land it back on a ship in any weather, day or night. In fact, Jerry and his fellow navy fliers didn't even call themselves pilots. They were better. They were *naval aviators*—air warriors—and they were invincible.

Jerry and his bombardier-navigator, Bill Tschudy, conducted their preflight checks. Then Jerry gingerly worked the throttles to taxi the Intruder toward the bow, past the ship's massive

3

superstructure, which bore a white "62," marking *Independence* as America's sixty-second aircraft carrier. A series of air crewmen in brightly colored shirts, goggles, and headphones guided Jerry to the catapult. Several men locked the Intruder into the mechanism that would momentarily drag the plane down the deck and sling it off the bow as if it weighed nothing.

Jerry Denton sat at the tip of a mighty spear. In his aircraft, he became an instrument of foreign policy. All the efforts of the United States Navy ultimately went toward launching him from this ship so he could drop bombs on an enemy target. Countless instructors had spent long hours training him. Veteran captains commanded their destroyers, submarines, and frigates to protect Jerry's aircraft carrier. Every man aboard *Independence* played a role in launching this heavy-laden plane off the deck with Jerry at the controls. Jerry and his fellow aviators existed at the very center of a loud, expensive, and highly dangerous enterprise.

Many flight instructors warned students their aircraft would try to kill them; pilots were always battling both their machines and physics. Especially in the 1950s and 1960s, they often lost. During Jerry's early career, longtime aviators had a 23 percent chance of dying in a crash; nearly half could expect an emergency ejection. Yet these men each felt in total control and ascribed any crash to a mistake. Jerry Denton didn't make mistakes. He always came home.

From his cockpit, Jerry looked to his left and saw a yellow-shirted officer spinning his hand in the air, signaling for full power. Jerry pushed the throttle forward. Behind him, his

Commander Jeremiah Denton with his A-6 Intruder aboard USS *Independence*, June 1965.

engines thundered. The Intruder bucked against the locked catapult. Jerry checked his rudder, elevators, and ailerons—the surfaces that controlled his aircraft's flight. All functioned perfectly. He gave a quick salute to the officer: He was ready. Jerry gripped the yoke with his left hand and the throttle with his right. The officer dropped to one knee and pointed his hand down the deck, giving the signal to launch. The catapult engaged. It yanked the Intruder forward and, three seconds later, slung it off the deck at 150 knots, or 170 miles per hour.

Four months earlier, in March 1965, the US military launched Operation Rolling Thunder, an air campaign designed to drop so many bombs on North Vietnam that its government would

5

cease supporting Communist insurgents in South Vietnam. The operation was part of America's strategy to support South Vietnam and contain Communism, the political system the American government perceived as the nation's greatest threat. The administration of President Lyndon Johnson believed in the Domino Theory—that Communism would topple democratic governments like dominoes, one after another, expanding the influence of China and the Soviet Union country by country across Southeast Asia and the globe. Granted, the government supported by the United States in South Vietnam was neither democratic nor popular, but at least it wasn't under the influence of Communist powers. Vietnam had become the latest proxy conflict in the Cold War between the United States and Soviet Union.

Jerry had flown more than twenty Rolling Thunder missions since arriving off the North Vietnamese coast in June 1965, and he grew more frustrated with each assignment. President Johnson and Secretary of Defense Robert McNamara permitted bombing only of certain targets as they tried to deter and intimidate North Vietnam without escalating the conflict into an all-out war. They often selected targets like parking lots, bridges, and depots instead of strategic bases, factories, and ports. Jerry and his squadron mates felt they routinely risked their lives for little gain. Thus far, Rolling Thunder had not deterred the government of Communist Party Chairman Hồ Chí Minh in Hanoi. North Vietnam continued to support Communist guerrillas—known as Việt Cộng—in South Vietnam. By the end of 1965, America would have committed nearly two hundred thousand troops to the growing conflict.

From his cockpit, Jerry could see little difference between North and South Vietnam. His shadow flicked over flooded fields of rice in North Vietnam that looked just like paddies south of the Demilitarized Zone, or DMZ—the no-man's-land that separated the two countries just south of the seventeenth parallel. He quickly found the Mã River and followed it inland toward his target, the Than Hóa Bridge, which the North Vietnamese used to pump supplies south to the Việt Cộng.

"Rainbow flight from Rainbow leader," Jerry radioed to the twenty-seven aircraft arrayed behind him. "Target at ten o'clock . . . Rainbow leader rolling in."

Jerry pushed the yoke forward and nosed the Intruder toward the bridge and nearby battery of antiaircraft artillery. His bombardier-navigator, Bill Tschudy, readied the ordnance. Suddenly, an explosion shook the aircraft. Flames and smoke enveloped its wing. Warning lights flashed; the radio went dead. Another hit. The plane jerked and rolled right. Jerry stood up in his seat and jammed the left rudder pedal with such force that he snapped a tendon in his leg. Adrenaline masked the pain. The plane kept rolling. The engines stopped responding. Jerry lost control. He feared only seconds remained until the aircraft combusted.

When the Intruder righted itself momentarily, Jerry punched Tschudy in the shoulder: Time to eject, he signaled. Both men pulled their ejection handles. Tiny charges blew off the canopy, and a second later, Jerry and Bill rocketed upward in their ejection seats. They left the air-conditioned quiet of the cockpit and entered a hot cloudless sky boiling with explosions and alive with noise. Jerry tumbled through the air until his parachute deployed. He hung limply beneath a canvas dome and looked about. He watched his crippled aircraft flying away trailing thick smoke. He saw Bill in the distance beneath an open chute. Below him, the lightly forested ground, rapidly filling with infantry, came closer. Falling from one world into another, Jerry felt like Alice in Wonderland.

Seconds before Jerry lost his aircraft, he planned to complete another routine bombing run and return to *Independence* for a gluttonous evening meal served on linen tablecloths followed by a steaming shower. He'd sleep in fresh sheets before the next day's change-of-command ceremony, where he'd assume leadership of the Sunday Punchers. He'd arrive home in Virginia Beach by Christmas.

One explosion changed everything. It shredded two decades of confidence and rendered his considerable ability and status as a naval aviator irrelevant. His sense of invulnerability crumbled. During the thirty seconds he estimated he had before landing, he thought of evasion and escape.

Looking down, he observed that he'd land in the Mã River, which appeared muddy enough to hide his swimming downstream underwater. He'd splash down, the chute would collapse on top of him, and he'd strike out below the surface, swimming hard and surfacing far downstream. He'd hide in riverbank bushes, lying submerged and breathing through a hollow reed overnight. The next day, he'd make his way to the coast—only ten miles away—and signal for a rescue. He'd be flying missions again by next week.

Below him, uniformed enemy troops lined the riverbank. They watched him float helplessly toward them. His descent seemed to accelerate as he neared the river and his feet plunged into the muddy water. His whole body followed. The limp parachute settled just upstream. Below the surface, Jerry quickly freed himself from the straps and kicked off, heading downstream.

With sudden horror, he realized his left leg wouldn't move. Until now, he hadn't noticed the severity of his injury. He had a ruptured tendon that, after the rough ejection, now protruded through a gash in his skin and flight suit. His left leg was useless. His heavy flight boots began pulling him downward, into the river's cold depths. Panic replaced calm. Jerry kicked for the surface and gasped for air. He swallowed water and choked. He gasped and began sinking; his boots were too heavy. In that moment, survival became more important than escape. He inflated his life vest and shot to the surface. Looking around, he could see soldiers watching him from the bank. They waved him toward shore; one fired a shot over Jerry's head. No options remained except surrender. He could imagine nothing worse.

Soldiers dragged Jerry from the brown water and stripped him of every item he had except his underwear. They took his flight suit, boots, socks, weapon, radio, and watch. They left him wet, muddy, injured, nearly naked, and bound with rope. The accomplished naval aviator and father of seven struggled to retain his pride. He felt much less like an American officer than he had moments earlier.

Kneeling amid a gaggle of thirty soldiers, he first wondered when, if, or in what condition he'd return to his family. He had no real idea what might lie before him. Truthfully, he knew little about North Vietnam and even less about how the North Vietnamese treated American prisoners. He suddenly thought about what would sustain him through whatever lay ahead. He recalled a list of important quotations he'd kept during his college years at the Naval Academy. Now, facing an unknown test, several came back to him. "Nurture your mind with great thoughts," Benjamin Disraeli had said. "To believe in the heroic makes heroes."

Jerry also recalled an anonymous quote that seemed apropos: "The greatest heroes known are those that are afraid to go, but go." Jerry was certainly afraid; he didn't have much choice about going, however. He could only control *how* he went, *how* he would conduct himself. He could choose *how* to respond to whatever came. Despite all he'd lost, he remained a man of faith and a naval officer. He resolved to show North Vietnam what that meant.

Chapter 2

HỎA LÒ PRISON

JERRY UNCEREMONIOUSLY ENTERED Hanoi in the back of a jeep. His captors had blindfolded him on the riverbank, and since then he'd caught only narrow glimpses of roads, villages, and jeering citizens. Yet he knew he had arrived in North Vietnam's capital city. He could smell it: the food, fumes from cars and trucks, garbage, and sewage. His guards, weary from the night's drive, paid him little attention, and he adjusted the blindfold so he could see. He knew enough about Vietnamese history to understand the French influence he saw in the city's architecture.

France had colonized Vietnam and renamed it French Indochina in 1887; Hanoi had been the seat of colonial government. The country remained a colony until Hồ Chí Minh, then a young Vietnamese nationalist, led Vietnam to independence in 1954. Victory had followed the eight-year Indochina War between Hồ Chí Minh's Việt Minh forces and France's colonial army. The United States had heavily subsidized France, its ally in the Cold War against Communism and the Soviet Union.

11

Despite the United States funding more than half the French war effort, France lost. The Geneva Conference of 1954 ended the war along with France's colonial rule. The treaty temporarily divided Vietnam in two, ceding the northern half to the Communist Việt Minh and the south to the regime of former emperor Bảo Đại. The peace agreement called for a single national election within two years.

Before a year had passed, the United States government helped Bảo Đại's prime minister oust Bảo Đại himself. Ngô Đình Diệm thus came to power in Saigon and founded the Republic of Vietnam (South Vietnam), which was a republic in name only. The autocratic Diệm and his American supporters knew a national election would give Hồ Chí Minh power over all Vietnam, so they declined to hold the referendum. Conflict between the Republic of Vietnam and the Democratic Republic of Vietnam (North Vietnam) was assured. The Việt Cộng began an insurgent campaign to topple the regime in South Vietnam and unite the country. Hồ Chí Minh's government in Hanoi heavily supported these guerrilla fighters, while Presidents Eisenhower, Kennedy, and Johnson steadily increased US military backing for Diệm's regime. By 1964, more than 23,000 US troops were deployed in South Vietnam, albeit as noncombat advisors. Their noncombat status changed in August of 1964.

President Johnson seized upon a murky naval incident off the North Vietnamese coast and dubiously claimed North Vietnam had repeatedly attacked American vessels. He used the episode to rally support for direct American intervention in Vietnam. Patriotism and anticommunism ran high in Washington and the resulting Gulf of Tonkin resolution passed 416–0 in the US House of Representatives and 88–2 in the Senate on August 7, 1964, just three days after the incident itself. The resolution broadly authorized the president to send American planes, ships, and men directly into combat against Communist forces in Southeast Asia—and do so without a formal congressional declaration of war. Thus, with little oversight from Congress, the Johnson administration began rapidly increasing troop levels in South Vietnam. The administration also initiated the Operation Rolling Thunder air campaign against North Vietnam. The president and his advisors aspired to defeat the insurgency in South Vietnam, break North Vietnam's will to support the Việt Cộng, and halt the spread of Communism. The public seemed confident victory would come quickly. Jerry had seen France lose its war in Vietnam just eleven years earlier; he hoped the Johnson administration would not similarly underestimate the determination of Vietnamese guerrillas and Hồ Chí Minh. Jerry had to trust the president had a winning strategy.

Through glimpses beneath his blindfold, he saw tree-lined boulevards reminiscent of Europe. They carried a mix of mostly bicycle and pedestrian traffic. Periodically, he spotted manicured gardens and parks. As Jerry well knew, US policy prohibited attacks on Hanoi, and the city hummed along undisturbed. A noticeable number of military trucks offered the only hint of war.

The jeep turned off a main artery onto a quiet side street. On his right, Jerry saw a long yellow stucco wall at least fifteen feet high. Shards of glass lined the top. Over the glass ran lines of wire. The wall seemed impenetrable from without. Carved over its one portal were the words *Maison Centrale*, a French term Jerry knew meant "prison." He gulped. He feared this was his destination and that it would prove as inescapable as its wall was impermeable.

As the jeep idled outside the gate, Jerry suddenly felt a handbag smash into his face. He shook off his surprise and lifted his nose to see a Vietnamese woman with a purse briskly walking away. Aviators flying high above hostile lands never saw the citizens their bombs affected; they remained largely immune from the personal consequences of war. An unlucky explosion had changed that reality for Jerry. He lost his immunity the moment he ejected from his aircraft. For the first time in his life, he feared the personal anger of foreign citizens. He worried far worse treatment awaited him inside the imposing walls where he would be at the mercy of North Vietnam.

The gates soon groaned open, and the jeep rolled through them. Jerry heard the echoes of a tunnel followed by the quiet of a courtyard. The jeep stopped. Guards lifted Jerry out and walked him back toward the entrance, then ushered him to the right. He entered a drafty corridor. As he shuffled along blindfolded, he heard "Yankee Doodle" whistled low and mournfully. A small burst of hope ran through his body. At least another American is here, Jerry thought. Perhaps his bombardier-navigator, Bill Tschudy, would be here too.

Part of being an untouchable naval aviator involved paying little attention to the tragedies or failures that combat inevitably brings. Consequently, Jerry did not know how many Americans North Vietnam had captured since the air war Operation Rolling Thunder began in March of 1965. He'd been vaguely familiar with Ev Alvarez, the first American captured. Younger Naval Academy graduates Bob Shumaker and Phil Butler had also been downed north of the DMZ, as had a World War II air force vet named Guarino. Other than that, he knew little about who or what he might encounter as a prisoner of war in North Vietnam.

Like all pilots and aviators, Jerry had received training in survival, evasion, resistance, and escape—SERE, they called it. The course taught officers how to survive behind enemy lines or in captivity. The navy based its training on one constant: the rules established by the 1949 Geneva Convention relative to the Treatment of Prisoners of War. The agreement outlined humane treatment for POWs and defined what captors could and could not ask a prisoner. Mainly, POWs had to give only their name, rank, service number, and date of birth; Americans called these the Big Four. Any other information was off-limits. Captors also had to treat prisoners humanely. The United States, North Vietnam, and 102 other countries had signed the treaty.

The American military also developed its own code governing conduct of captured servicemembers. Jerry Denton and countless other men had committed the principles of its six articles to memory. If an unexpected situation ever created doubt about how to act, an American could fall back on the Code of Conduct.

CODE OF CONDUCT FOR MEMBERS OF THE ARMED FORCES OF THE UNITED STATES

ARTICLE I

I am an American fighting man. I serve in the forces which guard my country and our way of life. I am prepared to give my life in their defense.

ARTICLE II

I will never surrender of my own free will. If in command, I will never surrender my men while they still have the means to resist.

ARTICLE III

If I am captured, I will continue to resist by all means available. I will make every effort to escape and aid others to escape. I will accept neither parole nor special favors from the enemy.

ARTICLE IV

If I become a prisoner of war, I will keep faith with my fellow prisoners. I will give no information or take part in any action which might be harmful to my comrades. If I am senior, I will take command. If not, I will obey the lawful orders of those appointed over me and will back them up in every way.

ARTICLE V

When questioned, should I become a prisoner of war, I am bound to give only name, rank, service number, and date of birth. I will evade answering further questions to the utmost of my ability. I will make no oral or written statements disloyal to my country and its allies or harmful to their cause.

ARTICLE VI

I will never forget that I am an American fighting man, responsible for my actions, and dedicated to the principles which made my country free. I will trust in my God and in the United States of America.

For the moment, Jerry assumed North Vietnam would honor the Geneva Convention, and he concentrated on absorbing every detail of the old prison. Unfortunately, his tour ended after only thirty yards. His guard stopped him before a metal door, opened it, and pushed Jerry inside. The guard removed the blindfold, and Jerry observed a room approximately nine feet long and eight feet wide. Two raised concrete platforms served, presumably, as bunks. A barred window looked out onto an alleyway between the cellblock and the foreboding wall Jerry had seen upon arrival. He spied roaches darting into crevices. The guard motioned to a metal bucket in the corner; that was Jerry's latrine. He also saw a wooden block with two recessed arches affixed to the end of each bunk. A rusty, hinged metal bar with corresponding raised arches lay across the wooden block. Were these leg stocks? Surely, he thought, their use had ended along with French colonialism.

The guard also left clothes that looked like Valentine's Day pajamas to Jerry. They were long-sleeved, thin, baggy, and had broad red-and-pink vertical stripes. With a gesture, the guard

17

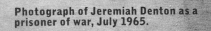
Photograph of Jeremiah Denton as a prisoner of war, July 1965.

ordered him to put on the clothes, then locked Jerry behind the heavy door. Jerry looked disdainfully at his new outfit. At least the clothes were clean, and he put them on. Dressed, he found himself alone for the first time since being shot down. He was exhausted. He lay on a hard bunk and fell asleep. Perhaps he'd wake up aboard *Independence* and find Hanoi had been nothing but a bad dream.

The voice that awakened him did not belong to an American. In surprisingly good English, a North Vietnamese guard roused Jerry and informed him he was to be interrogated. Jerry indicated he felt terrible and couldn't walk. He pointed to the snapped tendon that had popped through the skin on his left thigh. "I can't walk," he said. A second guard applied a bayonet point, and Jerry got moving on his hands and knees.

He crawled along several passageways. He entered a room numbered "18" and found two officers seated behind a desk. They indicated Jerry should sit on the low stool before them. He took his seat and glared at the officers, hoping a look of pride would mask his fear. For all his confidence, he had no weapons, no friends of influence, and no real protection from whatever his captors wished to do.

One officer wore civilian clothes and introduced himself as a student of history and literature. Jerry guessed he was about thirty. The other might have been forty and wore an unmarked military uniform; he claimed to be a pilot. They informed him he had arrived at Hỏa Lò Prison in Hanoi; the name, he learned, was pronounced "wah-lo." They explained that the building had been constructed by the French to house Vietnamese prisoners during more than fifty years of unjust colonial occupation.

They asked Jerry his basic information and he politely answered, giving them his name, rank, service number, and date of birth, as permitted by the Geneva Convention and Code of Conduct. Then the civilian asked, "What kind of plane were you flying?"

The A-6 Intruder was the navy's newest aircraft, and Jerry had already fretted over how his captors might ply him for information about the new jet. He had vowed not to divulge its capabilities. Instead, he answered by repeating his name, rank, service number, and date of birth; the Geneva Convention required nothing more and the Code of Conduct bound him to surrender only those four pieces of information. The two interrogators kept at it for ten minutes. Jerry kept up his resistance, and eventually they sent the new prisoner back to his cell with their questions unanswered. Jerry was so exhausted, he later could not recall if he'd walked or crawled back to his cell, or if he'd been carried. He fell asleep once again.

After he awoke, he discovered his new diet. Guards brought him lukewarm phở, soup with stringy greens and various scraps of meat, fat, and vegetables. They fed him twice a day; his stomach rarely stopped growling. His 6-foot, 167-pound body needed more.

For several days, Jerry slept when he could and faced off against the interrogators when he had to. The pair continued battering him with questions: "Where were you born?" "What aircraft carrier were you on?" "What bomb load did your plane carry?" Jerry parried them all, answering with name, rank, service number, and date of birth as best he could. If he said something else, he made it innocuous or false.

The interrogators grew as weary as their prisoner. Finally, the civilian said, "If you continue to refuse to cooperate in a reasonable way by answering our questions, we cannot guarantee your safety. If you continue to insult us, we will have to turn you over to the civilian authorities, who will force you to talk."

"If we turn you over to the civilians, they will apply severe punishment," the other elaborated. "If that punishment results in losing a limb, they will dispose of you. They would not want to send you home a cripple."

Jerry raised his voice and said, "Are you daring to make threats against my life in contravention of the Geneva Conventions?"

His adversaries conferenced and decided to dismiss their prisoner. But they left him with a worrisome warning. The Geneva Convention did not bind them in this situation, they explained. The United States had not declared war on North Vietnam. Thus, they could treat the Americans as war criminals who'd attacked their villages and people. The prisoners should not jeopardize the leniency they'd experienced to date; the North Vietnamese people could, if they wished, try them in court. Jerry, whose leg remained untreated, was not impressed with North Vietnam's mercy and hospitality so far, and he felt certain America would protect him. Yet he limped back to his cell nervously wondering what this legal perspective might mean.

Jerry had heard one American whistling when he first arrived in Hỏa Lò Prison. He knew a good whistle would carry through his brick, stone, and concrete environs, but he'd also been ordered and threatened not to communicate in any way—and he believed the guards' threats. After two days of silent, isolated residence, he couldn't stand being quiet any longer. Near his window, he began softly whistling "Anchors Aweigh," the Naval Academy fight song. Maybe an American would hear him.

Shortly, Jerry heard, "Hello, Yank!" The voice drifted through his window from somewhere down the alleyway between the cellblock and yellow exterior wall. Jerry guessed the voice came from two or three cells down the row.

Jerry replied, "Yeah." He was skeptical. Could it be a trick?

"What's your name," the voice asked.

"This is Jerry Denton, US Navy. Who are you?"

"Guarino, major, Air Force."

Jerry recognized the name; he could trust this voice. "Oh . . . yeah, I heard of you," he said. "The Vietnamese released your name as captured."

"No kidding? That's great news, Jerry," Larry Guarino replied. "What kind of airplane were you flying?"

Jerry laughed. "That's what *they'd* like to know!"

"I bet you're from Canoe U," Guarino said, meaning the Naval Academy.

"That's right! How are they treating you?"

"Oh, they aren't treating me too badly."

"Well, don't worry," Jerry said with confidence. "We'll hack 'er." He thought a moment, then asked, "How many men have been repatriated so far?"

"Never heard of *anybody* being repatriated" came Guarino's reply.

"How's the mail been coming through?"

"Don't be ridiculous, Jerry. We don't get any mail up here."

"Well, don't worry about it," Jerry reiterated with slightly less confidence. "We'll hack 'er."

Jerry and Larry Guarino began talking and whistling to each other, more and more overtly. Eventually, the prison staff noticed. "You are absolutely forbidden to speak or make any sounds," one officer warned the pair. "You must only sit and ponder your crimes against the Vietnamese people!" From his interrogation sessions, Jerry had gathered that the French had imprisoned several current North Vietnamese prison officials in this very dungeon; the North Vietnamese knew exactly how prisoners thought. Consequently, they knew the value of keeping POWs isolated. The captors wanted prisoners to become desperate little islands, lonely and susceptible to coercion.

The two Americans kept communicating. Soon, Guarino felt he knew Jerry well enough to confess his real situation. "Jerry," he finally said, "I'm in bad shape. They are giving me almost nothing to eat. I'm down to a hundred pounds and I haven't crapped in twenty-six days. I don't remember how long I've been in irons, but it's been weeks. I don't know whether I can make it."

Guarino's report shocked Jerry; he asked for an explanation. "I think it was because I was impolite at one of the quizzes," Guarino said. Jerry assumed *quizzes* referred to interrogations. "I lost my temper and spilled a cup of tea all over the table. I was only giving them name, rank, service number, and date of birth. They threatened me about that but didn't do anything until I spilled the tea. Guess they thought I was being rude." Jerry made a note to keep his temper in check.

For several days, Jerry's world inside Hỏa Lò Prison comprised just his cell and Room Eighteen. Chats with Larry Guarino became his only friendly contact. He burned to know who else lived nearby. Eventually, guards took him to a latrine in the far corner of the small courtyard; his world nearly doubled in size. Inside the latrine, he learned toilets in North Vietnam consisted of a hole in the cement. That at least beat the rusty bucket inside his cell. He used the facilities quickly as the summer heat, humidity, and stench made the interior unbearable. Outside, the guard allowed him to wash his red-and-pink pajamas, which he thought of as his clown suit. He hung them to dry in the hot sun. The guard motioned to a pail of water and indicated Jerry should wash. Given the primitive conditions, he wasn't quite sure of the procedure, so he poured the entire bucket over himself. He looked up rather pathetically, water trickling down his face and body. His guard burst out in laughter.

Jerry's trips to the latrine became more frequent in the coming days, and he learned to use his bucket of water more judiciously.

On his way to wash one day, Jerry heard a soft voice coming from a door on the north side of the courtyard. "Go fishing," it said.

Once inside the latrine, Jerry spied a matchstick placed across a metal drain. He lifted it up and found a tiny roll of paper dangling from a string tied around the match. He unrolled the note. It read, "Welcome to the Hanoi Hilton. If you read this, spit as you depart the latrine door. Shumaker, USN."

Jerry knew of Bob Shumaker; he'd been the second American captured in North Vietnam. Jerry couldn't help but smile at the nickname his fellow aviator had given the prison. Jerry spat emphatically when he walked out of the latrine to signal he'd read the note. Back in his cell, he quickly set about establishing a dialogue and borrowed Shumaker's technique. He scavenged a burnt match, which he wet and used to write on the rough brown toilet paper issued to the POWs. He began to communicate via note drops in the latrine.

Between his conversations with Major Larry Guarino and note drops with Lieutenant Commander Shumaker, Jerry soon confirmed he outranked everyone else in captivity. As of July 31, 1965, that number included seventeen POWs. To his relief, he had learned his bombardier-navigator, Bill Tschudy, was among them; he'd worried Tschudy might not have survived the trip to Hanoi. Their captors had placed the Americans in two sections of Hỏa Lò. Shumaker and other early arrivals had nicknamed Jerry's section New Guy Village; Jerry had heard that Heartbreak Hotel lay somewhere deeper inside the prison.

Following the Code of Conduct, Jerry took command. He issued his first orders via note drop in the New Guy Village latrine: "Follow the Code of Conduct. Think about escape. I want a note about it every day, and I want a map of the camp." He immediately thought back to those quotes he'd memorized about heroism. He realized his little army didn't need a hero; it needed a leader. Jerry believed he should set the example. He knew Article III of the Code of Conduct required he make every effort to escape, so he designed a plan. Ignoring the obvious challenge of scaling the prison's menacing wall and navigating the streets of Hanoi and roads of the North Vietnamese countryside, Jerry decided to pry the bars off his window and bust out of the Hanoi

Hỏa Lò Prison, the "Hanoi Hilton," looking east by southeast. New Guy Village is top right.

Hilton. He broke off a piece of rusted iron from the leg stocks and chipped away the concrete that held the iron bars and framing in place. Day by day, he made progress. Every bit of concrete he chiseled from the wall gave him immense satisfaction and more encouragement.

One day, Jerry returned from a "quiz" to find guards inspecting his cell. They were furious. They confronted him with the improvised crowbar, loose window frame, and busted concrete. They manhandled him onto a bunk and locked his right ankle in the stocks. They left his injured leg unrestrained, which he at first appreciated. Over time, however, it rubbed against the rusted iron and became infected. The barbaric confinement raised Jerry's ire. For a while, he refused to eat.

From his bunk, he could still raise Guarino. He let several days pass without mentioning his new situation. Then, knowing guards had clamped Guarino in leg irons as well, Jerry asked, "Larry, I've been thinking about it for three days, but can't figure it. How do you take a crap in irons?"

"Aw heck, that's a long story," Guarino said back. "You don't want to hear it."

"Yeah, I'm really interested. How do you manage it?"

Grudgingly, Guarino explained his process to Jerry. "Now what did you want to know all that for?"

"Because I've been in these stocks for three days," Jerry revealed, "and I couldn't figure it out!" The surprising response drew a laugh from Guarino. Moments of humor kept American spirits afloat inside the Hanoi Hilton.

During long afternoons in solitary, Jerry thought back on different moments in his life. Confronted with the prospect of leading Americans in Hanoi, he recalled his first brush with leadership. One day in 1936, Jerry and several fellow eighth-grade boys were eating lunch outside of St. Mary Catholic School in Mobile, Alabama. Jerry had an infectious spirit of adventure and he suggested the boys use their lunch hour to explore a nearby culvert that led to a swampy woodland.

"Let's take off and go to the creek," said Jerry. The boys just laughed, but he persisted. "If we leave right now, we can have some fun." Convinced, the other boys set off behind Jerry. The rest of the class followed. Jerry guided twenty-five eighth-grade

Leg stocks used at Hỏa Lò Prison.

boys and girls through a dark culvert that ran beneath a street and led to a veritable jungle. The students fanned out to explore the woodland; nobody minded the time. When some students realized they'd been gone far longer than an hour, Jerry calmed them down. "School lets out in another hour. And we're already in as much trouble as we can get in. Why not enjoy the rest of the afternoon? Then we go straight home. The whole class won't be expelled."

Sister Mary Josephine called the entire eighth grade into the auditorium the next morning. She soon learned Jerry Denton had organized the unsanctioned expedition. She took him to her office and spoke with him for an hour. He never forgot the conversation. "It takes leadership to do what you've done," she explained. "If you have that much influence over people, you had better be very careful how you use it!"

He hoped he still had that gift. He certainly needed it now as he assumed leadership of the Americans in Hanoi. He hoped he wouldn't disappoint Sister Mary Josephine.

Larry Guarino and others passed Jerry's directives along as best they could to all known POWs in the camp. Jerry began formulating other guidelines he believed would help the POWs remain unified against their captors during this ordeal, which he guessed might last six months, perhaps more.

When he learned Larry Guarino had stolen a pencil from Room Eighteen, Jerry asked him to leave it in the latrine. Jerry picked it up on his next visit. Using an old razor blade, Jerry sharpened the pencil and began writing orders on sheets of toilet paper.

His first posted directive again reminded all POWs to abide by the Code of Conduct. In Jerry's mind, the six articles boiled down to this: American POWs should not cooperate with captors; should always think of escape; should assume the responsibility of command when necessary; and should give interrogators only their name, rank, service number, and date of birth for as long as possible. Perhaps most importantly, under Article V, they were bound not to make disloyal statements. Jerry set about running his prison like a military unit, despite their circumstances. His next set of orders included more specific policies:

1. FOLLOW THE CODE OF CONDUCT.

2. COMMUNICATE BY ALL MEANS AVAILABLE.

3. LEARN ALL POW NAMES AND LOCATIONS.

4. COMPLAIN ABOUT FOOD AND CONDITIONS.

5. GATHER MATERIALS LIKE WIRE, NAILS, AND PAPER.

6. OBSERVE A WEEKLY SUNDAY DEVOTIONAL PERIOD.

7. DO NOT ATTEMPT ESCAPE WITHOUT OUTSIDE HELP.

8. DO NOT ANTAGONIZE THE GUARDS.

The latrine in New Guy Village soon became a communications hub, connecting the various cellblocks inside the Hilton. Sometimes men left notes for specific POWs. More often, visiting POWs read the same scroll of toilet paper. They'd locate and unroll it when they ducked inside the latrine. They'd roll it up and replace it when they left. Each successful broadcast provided the men with a small victory over their captors. Jerry added new directives to the scroll on a regular basis. He felt each directive helped to remind the men they were military officers on a mission, not criminals as their captors so often called them. He refused to let his men become purposeless victims.

———

Importantly, Jerry found one note from Shumaker with a five-by-five matrix. The only writing said, "POWs learn this code."

	1	2	3	4	5
1	A	B	C/K	D	E
2	F	G	H	I	J
3	L	M	N	O	P
4	Q	R	S	T	U
5	V	W	X	Y	Z

Jerry realized Shumaker had established a language POWs could use to communicate covertly when they couldn't write, whisper, or send visual signals—which was most of the time, thanks to the hawklike watchfulness of guards. He learned Shumaker had named the method the Smitty Harris Tap Code, after an air force POW who'd recalled learning the code from a Korean War POW during survival training. To send a letter, POWs would tap the number corresponding to the letter's row, then tap the number corresponding to its column. For example, to send "B," Jerry would tap once for the letter's row, then twice for its column. He'd communicate C as "tap—quick pause—tap, tap, tap." The process seemed daunting and painstaking at first, but with hours of time on his hands, Jerry soon became proficient. To amplify sounds between cells, Jerry placed his metal cup to the wall and pressed his ear to the cup. He improved efficiency by using abbreviations, sending "GM" for *good morning*, and "GN" for *good night*. Translating taps into letters and strings of letters into words kept his mind sharp in the absence of other stimulation; most POWs soon had calloused knuckles. Guards realized the POWs were communicating via taps, but they couldn't break the code. Instead, they did their best to stifle the encrypted chatter. POWs had to remain vigilant; Jerry learned that getting caught tapping could bring a beating.

For a time, twenty-five-year-old navy POW Ed Davis occupied a New Guy Village cell that adjoined Jerry's. In the evenings when guards were scarce, Ed would croon "Fly Me to the Moon," by

Frank Sinatra. The tune's heartfelt longing made Jerry think of his wife, Jane, and their happy times together. It reminded him how much he loved her. He hoped she would wait for him.

Jerry and Davis became as close as two men could be, given they couldn't see each other and guards forbade overt communication. The tap code became their language. Once, Jerry heard Ed calling him on the wall with the usual five-beat "shave-and-a-haircut" sequence. Jerry tapped back twice: "two bits," the go-ahead confirmation. He put his cup to the plaster and listened. Using the tap code, Ed indicated he'd hidden a gift for Jerry in the latrine in honor of the Feast of the Assumption of Mary, on August 15; Ed knew Jerry was a devout Catholic. Jerry found the gift on his next visit: a cross woven from bamboo fiber that Jerry guessed Ed had pulled from a broom. Jerry had no other personal possession in Hanoi, and he treasured the cross. He hid it inside a propaganda pamphlet stuck under his pallet. He looked at it in private moments, and it gave him peace. It reminded him to seek strength in his boyhood faith.

One day in early fall 1965, when two guards entered Jerry's cell with a long piece of cloth, he immediately expected change. One guard watched Jerry while the other tied on the blindfold; Jerry hadn't been blindfolded since he arrived at Hỏa Lò three months earlier. The guards covered his upper body with a blanket, then hustled him out of his New Guy Village cell. No prying POWs could recognize his blanketed form moving through the prison's passageways; to them, Jerry would have simply disappeared. He wondered if he *was* disappearing. A gun barrel prodded him onto the floorboard of a vehicle. The engine started and the vehicle jerked into motion. He soon recognized the sounds of Hanoi's streets. He had no idea where they were taking him.

Chapter 3

THE ZOO

THE MOTOR STOPPED after what Jerry guessed was a twenty-minute drive that clearly took him away from downtown Hanoi. He noticed a relative quiet when a guard removed the blanket from his head and shoulders. He smelled a pungent aroma; when his blindfold was removed, he realized the scent came from an abandoned swimming pool filled with festering water. Jerry imagined mosquitoes would inflict worse harm than his jailors. Looking around, he saw nine buildings surrounding the pool. Boards or mats covered most windows. Weeds covered the grounds and livestock roamed untethered. Jerry surmised that the North Vietnamese military hadn't counted on hosting so many Americans and they'd run out of room at the Hilton. He'd arrived at a hastily improvised POW camp.

Guards walked him inside one of the buildings and shoved him into a small, hot, dark room. Jerry peered around his new cell. He saw a sheet of paper attached to the wall; it displayed the

35

camp rules, which reflected North Vietnam's disregard for the Geneva Convention:

All US aggressors caught red-handed in their piratical attacks against the Democratic Republic of Vietnam are criminals. While detained in this camp, you will strictly obey the following:

1. All criminals will bow to all officers and guards in the camp.

2. All criminals must show polite attitude at all times to the officers and guards in the camp, or they will be severely punished.

3. All criminals will answer questions orally or write any statement or do anything directed by the Camp Authority, or they will be severely punished.

4. Criminals are forbidden to attempt to communicate in any way, such as signals, tapping on the walls, attempting to communicate with criminals in the next room.

5. When in the bath area, do not attempt to communicate to any other criminals in the next area, or you will be severely punished.

6. Any criminal who attempts to escape, or helps others to do so, will be severely punished.

7. On the other hand, criminals who follow these camp regulations and who show a good attitude by concrete acts will be shown a humane treatment.

The sheet listed thirteen rules in total and was signed "Camp Authority." Jerry rolled his eyes at this Camp Authority's regulations. He duly set about communicating.

From other POWs, he soon learned the men had nicknamed this complex the Zoo; here POWs were the caged animals. The Americans had named individual buildings Barn, Stable, Pigsty, Chicken Coop, Auditorium, Pool Hall, Office, and Garage; Jerry was in Pool Hall. POWs called the swimming pool Lake Fester. Note drops in latrines and bathhouses were again common means of communication. Whispers carried information and jokes, but at greater risk. The Smitty Harris Tap Code was the predominant language. At times, the Zoo sounded like a den of woodpeckers, with POWs tapping out long messages to one another. Sometimes they passed orders. Other times, they were simply trying to pass time with conversation and to find human companionship.

Hours crept by at a glacial pace, especially in solitary confinement. The absence of visual or verbal human contact led Jerry's imagination to turn inward where memories would alternately inspire and haunt him. He fought temptation to linger on memories of his family. He tried mightily not to dwell on the irreplaceable time he was losing with them. Jerry prayed for them each morning and night, but otherwise he tried to focus elsewhere. He exhausted himself as he tried to keep memories of home at bay and struggled to overcome the creeping depression brought on by his miserable circumstance. He worried as much about his mind surviving this ordeal as he did his weakening body.

Jerry realized his rank made him senior ranking officer at the Zoo. As such, he rallied his men around the Code of Conduct. The code became more important when Jerry learned about the practices at the Zoo. Distance from Hanoi seemed to give interrogators more discretion. Fists, blows, and brutal isolation had become common techniques to extract information or statements. Rations were curtailed when prisoners refused to cooperate. Jerry learned Bob Shumaker had arrived at the Zoo before him and had already spent three weeks locked in a pitch-dark room as punishment for some perceived crime or offense. The Camp Authority had tired of American resistance.

Jerry knew his men needed rules and discipline, especially under these harsh circumstances. They needed to understand how to act and what to say when alone with interrogators. In the absence of written rules or a leader by their side to guide them through a quiz, they required a clear standard. Jerry emphasized the Code of Conduct, especially Article V. Every man knew the Code by heart and could consequently carry it into every interrogation.

Still, disagreements arose among the POWs about how to interpret the Code in their unique situation. Many reasoned giving innocuous or fake information did not violate the Code's spirit. Why should ill or injured men bring additional hardship on themselves by sticking to the literal requirement to say only name, rank, service number, and date of birth? POWs needed more food and fewer bruises. To Jerry, however, any compromise made POWs vulnerable to exploitation. Varying standards could wreck the unity so important to survival; men needed clear guidance. Jerry advocated a hard line: Make as few statements as possible beyond name, rank, service number, and date of birth. And if you say more, make them beat it out of you.

During this period, another aspiration began to percolate among the POWs. Leaders like Jerry Denton wanted their men to have a mental picture, not just rules, to take with them into a quiz. He wanted each man to imagine himself returning home with honor. Every man could then determine what actions would enable him to walk off a plane in America with his head held high, whenever that day came. Each man could determine what he needed to do in Hanoi so he could tell his family and fellow servicemen, "I did my best."

The POWs' motto and driving mission became "return with honor."

Two months had passed since Jerry's foot first became infected while he suffered in leg stocks, but it remained unhealed. The oozing blood and pus repulsed Jerry; he could scarcely look at his own foot. It grew worse, agitated by the slimy floors of latrines and bathhouses, along with the film of dirt covering everything at the Zoo. His foot's unsightly appearance did not inspire his captors to offer treatment or relief, however. The camp administrator still assigned him latrine duty.

That fall of 1965, the Zoo held some fifty-six prisoners yet had no sewer system; waste removal became a rotating job for POWs.

One evening, guards appeared at Jerry's door and motioned him outside. They instructed him to collect the latrine pails—"honeybuckets," as the POWs called them—left beside each cell door. He collected the stinking buckets from his cellblock and dumped their revolting contents into several larger buckets. He took the larger buckets to the edge of a field where POWs had placed buckets from other cellblocks. He'd have to dump them all. Two guards watched as he lifted two full buckets and began walking across the field to an open cesspool. The field had more weeds and debris than grass. Sticks, rocks, and shards of old metal made for an impossible minefield and pained Jerry's feet. The infection raging in his left foot accentuated the discomfort.

A twig splintered and cracked beneath his foot. A sharp rock nearly pierced his heel. Fuming, hurting, and humiliated, he labored onward. He eased himself down a nasty slope and emptied the two buckets into the cesspool. He climbed back to the field. He took several steps and another rock jabbed his foot. Pain shot up his leg. He threw down the empty buckets. Using his French, he turned to the guards and shouted, *"Fini, fini!"* He was done, and he was mad as hell.

One guard looked at Jerry and patted his pistol: *Get back to work.* Jerry didn't care. He yelled, "Bullshit!" In that moment, he'd had it. Enough with North Vietnam. Enough with this lousy prison camp. He walked straight through a second guard. The young soldier was so startled he dropped his rifle and stumbled backward. Jerry stalked fifty yards to his solitary cell. He never looked back. He slammed the door of his cell shut and fumed. Later that night, he heard a guard quietly lock his door.

The next day, the camp commander had Jerry's foot treated at last. It began to heal, helped by a surprisingly decent diet of cabbage, pumpkin soup, bread or rice, bananas, and occasional cast-off bits of chicken. The commander also installed two sawhorses in Jerry's cell to raise his sleeping pallet off the floor. Cockroaches would no longer scurry across his arms and legs at night. Jerry appreciated the care. While treatment was basic and restrictive, it became tolerable. Jerry could fall asleep feeling more human.

Fortune shifted the week of October 24. Jerry received messages indicating guards had caught POWs Ron Storz and Robbie Risner harboring contraband and drilling holes through walls so they could talk. Storz was thrown into solitary; Risner disappeared. Soon thereafter, angry guards burst into Jerry's cell for a shakedown. He watched helplessly as they found a bandage he'd been using as a tablet, a running list of known POWs, and a small piece of pencil lead. He watched, unable to stop them as they confiscated the list of names he'd worked so hard to create; now he'd have to start anew. Far worse, however, they discovered his cherished woven cross hidden inside a propaganda pamphlet. At bayonet point, Jerry watched with a sinking heart as a guard stomped on the cross, grinding it into the concrete floor with his boot. He threw away the shredded remnants. Jerry lost his only real possession. Now he had nothing.

Before guards led him away, Jerry saw a crew of North Vietnamese laborers enter his cell and begin bricking in the open transom above the door; communication would become even more difficult. He returned several hours later and immediately inventoried his cell; no sign of his tablet or scroll of POW names. The guards had left the propaganda pamphlet, and Jerry started to vent his anger by ripping it apart. Then he felt a slight bulge. He opened the pamphlet and found a new cross, woven from bamboo fibers. The gift overwhelmed him. He deduced that someone on the work detail had seen his cross trampled and, at substantial risk, fashioned him a new one. When he next poked out of his cell to pick up his food, several members of the detail were at work down the hallway. Jerry sent them a nod of thanks. He received a smile in return. The show of compassion lifted his spirits and steeled his faith.

On November 1, conditions grew worse. A guard opened Jerry's door at mealtime. Instead of the usual platter, Jerry saw a bowl of soup sitting in the dirt. He inspected it; it was cold and watery. Pieces of grit, specks of dirt, and two thin bits of cabbage floated on the surface. Disappointed, he picked out the grit, which he knew had caused cracked teeth among the POWs. Grit removed, he drank his morning meal. That evening, he found the same meager rations awaiting him. The food did not improve in the coming weeks. Jerry quickly withered to 120 pounds; he'd tipped the scales at a healthy 167 pounds on the day he was captured. Then the temperature plunged.

One late November morning, Jerry huddled in the corner of

his chilly cell. He'd wrapped his one thin blanket around himself as he slurped down his rations. He heard voices outside and the door opened. A delegation of North Vietnamese officials peered inside at the caged American leader, reminding Jerry exactly why POWs called this place the Zoo. He wished he could present a better figure than the skinny, dirty, hungry prisoner he'd become. He didn't look or feel much like a commanding officer.

"Well, Denton," one man began. "Do you know that you are eating shit?" The man may have intended the question as a joke, but Jerry had long suspected the dirt in his soup was human-based fertilizer. His own diarrhea, and that of other POWs, made him surmise the Camp Authority rarely washed vegetables before serving them. Starvation being the alternative, POWs ate every meal anyway.

Jerry didn't answer the question. The man asked loudly, "So you want to continue eating shit?"

Fury motivated Jerry to stand up. "Well, I hope there is some protein in it," he replied, struggling to his feet. The answer displeased the official. "You must condemn the policies of your government," he warned. "Until you do that, you will continue to eat shit!"

Food wasn't the only weapon applied to POWs that November. Jerry's neighbor, Ed Davis, the young lieutenant who'd originally woven Jerry's cross, suddenly stopped communicating. Jerry would tap again and again but never received a response. Then Jerry heard faint taps coming through the wall. It was Davis. Guards had cuffed his hands behind his back for refusing to provide any biographical information. He had to learn to tap and listen in his new configuration.

To support his friend, Jerry spent hours tapping to Davis. He often ended his messages with an imagined sponsorship plug: "Brought to you by the makers of Denton's Odorless Honeybuckets, the honeybucket with a lid . . ."

Ed's treatment worsened, but he held firm to the Code. Worried about Davis's well-being, Jerry tapped, "Maybe you should consider giving them some kind of answer, something that doesn't mean anything but will satisfy them."

"I don't think that way, sir," Davis replied.

"I just want you to consider the idea," tapped Jerry. "We have to find the best way to get you out of this situation."

The next time the interrogators came at him, Ed agreed to answer one question. He reported the exchange to Jerry.

His captors asked him, "When did you start school?"

"I started school when I was six years old," Davis confessed. The interrogators began asking him other questions, one after another. Davis didn't answer any of them. "You bastards," he fired back, "I told you I would answer *one* question. That's all."

He explained to Jerry, "I answered a question and it didn't stop anything. It was like, 'Now we've started and we can go from here.' Sir, it doesn't work!"

Both Jerry and Ed Davis were convinced the POWs needed to adhere to the hard line. They did, and Ed Davis suffered for it. A cadre of camp officials continued to hound Davis, demanding he sign an agreement promising to obey *their* orders, not those of Jeremiah Denton. They cut his food ration to a piece of bread and a cup of water each day. For a time, they even held back the bread.

Davis tapped that he now weighed around 110 pounds. He did not relent, however. He stuck by Jerry's orders to follow the Code of Conduct. He would not make any disloyal statements.

One night, Jerry heard guards enter Davis's cell. He listened to muffled thumps and occasional groans coming through the wall. Jerry heard Ed scream and thrash about in pain. Then came repetitive blows; Jerry guessed guards were beating Ed's head against his wooden sleeping pallet. Silence fell. Jerry heard a cell door shut and guards walking away. Then he heard scratching; Ed Davis was sending Morse code with a piece of metal. Davis scratched the wall for longs, or "dahs," and sent quick raps for shorts, or "dits."

POWs typically used the tap code, as longs or shorts were often difficult to send—and the North Vietnamese knew Morse code. Here, Davis's piece of metal made Morse possible, and nobody was listening; the guards were done with him for the night. Jerry engaged Davis with Morse, which he'd learned at the Naval Academy. It came back to him quickly and his ears were soon translating this old universal language of sailors and aviators.

Davis reported that the guards had roped up his arms behind him, pulling his shoulders and elbows back toward each other. It was his punishment for continuing to stonewall his interrogators. He tapped out one more word later that night as he suffered the aftereffects of torture: "Agony." Jerry had difficulty falling asleep knowing what his men suffered by following his orders. He'd heard about the ropes, straps, and bars employed by guards on uncooperative prisoners. He'd heard about broken men, devastated that they had been forced to surrender information or sign false statements. He wondered if he was leading these downed aviators wisely. Was his line too hard? Could they hack this brutality? No book, lecture, or quote had prepared him for this precise situation; no American fighting men had experienced something exactly like this. He had to trust his gut.

The next morning, Jerry heard sobbing through the wall. He tapped to Davis. In response, Davis scratched, "Commander, I've been doing some soul-searching. If I had it to do over again, maybe I could have just held out five minutes more." A sense of pride and validation filled Jerry Denton; tears welled in his eyes. His men believed in his leadership. Maybe he was doing the right thing.

He responded, "For God's sake, Ed, you did your best. You have nothing to be ashamed of. We are all proud of you. When they get around to the rest of us, I hope and pray we will do as well as you have."

On December 4, Jerry heard guards take Ed Davis away. He did not return.

Jerry wondered what would happen to the young lieutenant. He wondered if his own status as a senior officer, a full commander, intimidated the Camp Authority. Perhaps his rank kept the most severe torture at bay. He would willingly receive it; he needed to bear the same burdens his men did. He tried to guess when it would come.

The Camp Authority's agenda had become clear: They wanted to isolate prisoners, strip them of their pride, physically weaken them, and make them more pliable. If they could accomplish that, they could more easily cajole them for intelligence and information. Longer term, Jerry knew they'd go for confessions, political apologies, and propaganda statements. With every statement they forced, they figured the next statement would be easier to get. Eventually, they'd have a humiliated, guilty, demoralized, and very compliant population of prisoners—exactly what they needed to support North Vietnam's strategy.

Jerry knew the outgunned Communists could not beat the United States on the battlefield; he was sure Hồ Chí Minh knew it too. North Vietnam would instead try to swing public opinion against American involvement. If they could turn the American public and citizens in American-allied nations against the war with propaganda and statements from prisoners, they could hold out until America withdrew. The same statements would inspire North Vietnam's populace. A motivated North could easily conquer a weakened and abandoned South Vietnam. Jerry's leadership and the Code of Conduct had made the Camp Authority's relatively gentle approach to extracting propaganda ineffective to date. With no other options, the Camp Authority decided to employ harsher methods. Jerry knew he and his men would all suffer. He rallied POWs to their mission and *cause de la résistance*: returning home with honor. They were determined not to fail.

The POWs had nicknamed the commandant of the Zoo "Dog," and Jerry generally respected him. Dog spoke English well and seemed reasonable. He allowed POWs turkey and an extra blanket at Christmas and played a moving violin version of "Smoke Gets in Your Eyes" over the speakers placed throughout the camp; the familiar notes offered a welcome break from the propaganda broadcasts the speakers usually carried. Jerry began meeting with Dog more regularly. He hoped speaking commander-to-commander might spark progress. The two men soon became conversational; at some point a body could not just continue reiterating name, rank, service number, and date of birth. Jerry and other POWs found the human need for contact and connection too great to overcome entirely. Jerry at least tried to make his topics and words innocuous. More often than not, he fabricated his responses.

During one exchange in December, Dog wondered aloud if Jerry would like to write home. Jerry answered, "Yes." He did not know for certain if Jane knew he'd survived; a letter from him would change that. The prisoners suspected, correctly, that North Vietnam had not told the United States which POWs they'd captured. That dreadful prospect added one more nightmare to their dreams: *What if my family doesn't even know I'm alive?* POWs wanted desperately to write home.

"Well," Dog countered, "I am not sure that I will allow you to write. You have a bad attitude. What special reason do you have for wanting to write? Only those with special reasons are allowed to write."

"There is no special reason to write, but I have a wife and seven children and I want to tell them I am well."

"Ah," Dog said, clearly pleased he'd gained this new information. "We respect a man with seven children."

Then Dog presented his prisoner a pen and notepad; he gave Jerry a most unanticipated chance as a Christmas gesture. Jerry was both ecstatic and frightened. He had no time to prepare. What if he wrote the wrong thing? What would he mistakenly leave unwritten? How could he share his honest thoughts but not have his captors disapprove the letter? He had little chance to consider these questions; he just began writing, not knowing how much time he'd be permitted.

"My dearest wife and children," he began. "I am allowed to write you for Christmas, for which I am grateful. But it is impossible for me to cram into a book, much less a letter, the pent-up love I want to express to you all. This opportunity came as a surprise so I am not prepared to recall even the essential things I'd like to say.

"My Christmas gift to you all are the countless prayers I have said and will say for you," he continued, "and a poem composed since I came here:

My Jane

When God made her His mood was the finest
(Remembering His Own Mary's Grace)
He fashioned her brow for a love-hungry child
And for fortunate men, her face.

49

HE CREATED HER BODY FOR SCULPTURE
WITH HANDS THAT ARE GENTLE AS DOVES
AND EYES THE MOST BEAUTIFUL MIRRORS
OF A HEART FULL OF TENDER LOVES.

YES, HE ONLY MADE ONE LIKE MY JANIE
WHICH POSES A PROBLEM FOR ME
FOR HOW CAN I EVER REPAY HIM
FOR ENTRUSTING SUCH TREASURE TO ME?

"Darling, I am well in body, mind, and soul," the letter continued. "I've never been so close to God and I pray all day each day for you and the others dead and alive who have given so much for us.

Jane Denton and family.

"When I return my life will be better lived for Him and for you. This is not a promise but a fact."

He went on to share his hopes for his family's health, his children's schooling, even his worry that the rope for the backyard swing needed replacing. He poured out his love and his concern for a family unexpectedly left without him. He was grateful for the opportunity, even as remembering home saddened him. He went to sleep that night thinking of his family, what he wrote, and what he forgot to include.

A short time later a newly arrived POW told Jerry he'd heard about his statement. To Jerry's surprise and ire, the North Vietnamese had announced over Radio Hanoi that Jeremiah Denton would be glad when the war was over so he could return to his wife and seven children. His letter said nothing of the sort, but his captors had used his biographical information to make an antiwar advertisement! The news incensed Jerry. He was furious with Dog for being duplicitous and with himself for deviating from his own orders. He redoubled his efforts to resist. He'd let his defense down and been burned; from now on, he would stick to the hard line of defiance. He held himself up as an example and implored his men not to make his mistake.

The path of resistance became more unpleasant. Jerry had several onerous quizzes with his two adversaries from his early days in the Hanoi Hilton; he learned other POWs had nicknamed them "Eagle" and "Owl." He still refused to cooperate. He became more combative. He adhered tightly to the Code of Conduct, his one steadying touchpoint in this crazy world. He'd decided to follow its letter. Once he'd made that decision, compromise ceased being an option. He'd made his choice, and every action would back it up.

On February 7, 1966, Dog walked Jerry to a building called the Auditorium; two guards followed. Ominously, Dog said, "Your arrogant attitude is going to cause you a great deal of trouble, Denton." His statement worried Jerry. They entered the old theater, and the door shut loudly behind them. The sound echoed through the chilly, empty space. Dog led Jerry into the building, and their footsteps echoed like the doors. The forlorn sounds reminded Jerry of his complete isolation from his men and his former world. No American on earth knew where he was.

Dog asked once again if Jerry would write a biography, a summary of his personal history. Jerry refused. Dog looked at him as if he had lost his mind. He said, "There's nothing I can do then, Denton." He turned his back on Jerry and walked away, likely wondering why Americans chose severe punishment instead of writing the simple statements requested of them. Jerry knew Dog would never understand that his honor was all he had left. If he lost that, he'd have surrendered his identity. He'd lose the will to resist, survive, and even live. No, he would cling to his honor and the Code no matter what.

The two guards remained after Dog left. One gripped Jerry's shoulder and shoved him into a small closet. He could hardly see in its dark confines. Bamboo mats and thick blankets covered the one small window. Perhaps he could reach up and detach them once the guards left, he thought. Then he heard clanking metal. One guard pulled Jerry's hands behind his back and cuffed them. The other guard clamped irons around his legs. The irons consisted of metal loops that circled his ankles with a heavy bar connecting the two loops. Jerry could hardly see them for the darkness.

A guard asked if Jerry would write. Jerry said no. Immediately, a hard fist struck him square in the face. He fell. A guard hauled him back to his feet. Jerry felt another blow and sank down again into the darkness. The guard pulled him up and socked him once more. He felt warm blood trickle from his nose. The guard offered Jerry an exit: Would he write anything at all? Jerry categorically refused. The guard threw him into a corner. The soldiers left and locked the door behind them, leaving Jerry in blackness. He waited for his eyes to adjust. They couldn't. No light penetrated the walls, window, or door. Jerry could have been in the depths of a cave. He gradually became disoriented. With hands locked behind him, he scrunched along the floor, dragging the irons with him. He searched frantically for some relief from the blackness. At last, he found one faint filament of light that slipped through a minuscule crack in the door. It was his only visual reference. It would become Jerry's best friend. He spoke to it often. The little beam gave him company in the darkest and loneliest place he'd ever been.

Jerry suffered in darkness for, as best he could estimate, four days. He dwelled in an unending starless night; midnight and midday looked identical. His sense of time slipped away along with his sanity. The seeping winter coldness penetrated his thin rags and skinny body, settling into his very bones. His back and shoulders ached from having his arms folded behind him; the biting cuffs swelled his wrists and gradually restricted circulation to his hands. He lost feeling in them. Would he lose them altogether?

On that fourth day, a guard entered, turned on the light, and examined Jerry's hands. He grunted, left, and returned with three men. Together, they worked to release the cuffs, which had become virtually buried in Jerry's grotesquely swollen wrists. One cuff finally released. An officer arrived and uncharacteristically apologized to Jerry: "Denton, I am sorry about this."

For what seemed like hours, the three men worked at the second cuff. They finally disassembled it. It fell to the floor, and Jerry stared at his freed hands. They'd doubled in size; they were black as his cell had been. He wondered if he would ever be able to use them again. At least the interminable darkness was gone and other people were with him. Then suddenly, hands yanked his arms behind his back again, applied a new set of cuffs, and threw him into the corner. The guards disappeared along with the light.

The passing hours continued to tax his mind. It became a battlefield between determination and despondency, confidence and doubt. He imagined America's greatness. He drew upon that image and sense of pride to justify his sacrifice. His resistance mattered because American ideals mattered; he was confident he'd chosen the right path. Then doubt charged forward and his resolve retreated. "What difference does it make?" he asked himself. "Why not give in?" Otherwise, he might well die and nobody would even know he'd upheld his honor. He became a miserable, conflicted wreck.

He withered by the hour. Reality slipped away, replaced by disorientation. What day was it? Where was he? Who was he? Moments of lucidity came less often as days five and six passed by. Finally, during what he feared might be his last moments of sanity, he cried out. He had nothing left to give for himself or his country. He would write. Yes, he would write.

A guard opened the cell door. The blinding light came; Jerry squinted against the light bulb. He had reached his life's lowest point. He smelled of waste. His body had shrunken. His wrists still oozed pus. He had surrendered in shameful defeat. He felt like an embarrassment to his family and his country. How could he ever return home?

He didn't remember leaving the cell inside the Auditorium. He came to with Dog watching over him as he broke the Code of Conduct. Hell, he smashed it. He wrote a personal biography. He went far, far beyond the Big Four (name, rank, service number, and date of birth). Each additional word hurt. It ached to grip the pen. It hurt to move his hands over the paper. Yet it was nothing compared to the pain of breaking his own order. Little he wrote was true, but if the Camp Authority got something from him, perhaps they wouldn't send him back to that god-awful black hole. He couldn't last another day in its solitary horror.

Dog returned Jerry to the same cell, but under better conditions. When the guards placed him inside, they left his hands and ankles free. When the door shut, the light remained on. The cell had been cleaned. When the door opened later that day, a guard offered improved rations.

Slowly, Jerry began to heal. He realized no Americans at the Zoo knew his whereabouts. From what the guards told him, however, he knew Dog had waved his biography in front of other POWs. Dog aimed to humiliate Jerry, but he'd actually told the POWs that Jeremiah Denton was alive and still at the Zoo. Dog also inadvertently told the POWs that Jerry had surely endured horrific torture. Jerry hoped this knowledge would increase his men's resolve. As he pondered his ordeal, Jerry felt his own resolve increase too. His mind cleared and sharpened. His spiritual and physical strength returned. He'd reached his limits and still only surrendered a harmless, half-true biography. He considered the pain worthwhile. He prepared for another round.

Dog did not offer Jerry an immediate rematch. Several weeks passed by, with Jerry and all his renewed resolve squirreled away in the same tiny cell, alone and far removed from the other POWs in the Zoo. He might have bread, water, and soup, but he considered communication the real bread of a prisoner's life. He had no connection to anyone outside the Auditorium, and he turned inward again. Jerry dwelled once more in memories of St. Mary Catholic School, where his faith had originally been kindled. He visualized the brothers and sisters who taught him lessons about academics and the Lord. He imagined the classroom and recalled faces and names from elementary school as he walked himself down each row of desks. He stood in his Hanoi cell alongside his class in Mobile as they recited the Pledge of Allegiance together. He considered each word and they gave him strength. "I pledge allegiance to the flag of the United States of America, and to the republic for which it stands, one nation, under God, indivisible, with liberty and justice for all." By the time he graduated from St. Mary Catholic School, and later McGill Institute, a high school run by the Brothers of the Sacred Heart, he had a powerful faith in America and God. His patriotism and faith became a driving inner force. His imagined time with classmates helped fortify him for his inevitable return to reality.

One day in early March 1966, the door opened and guards pulled Jerry from his cell. They led him through the dim hallways of the Auditorium and out into the springtime. Fresh air swirled around him and he breathed deeply. He felt warmth on his face. Fifty yards later, he was back inside, walking down another dim corridor. At its end, guards pushed him into a new cell. Jerry heard the door lock and footsteps recede. He heard a whistle, then whispers in the hallway. Taps came through his wall: "Welcome to the Pool Hall."

Jerry surveyed his neighbors and found himself surrounded by other Americans, most of whom had roommates. Among them, he discovered POWs Fred Cherry and Porter Halyburton. He found their story fascinating. Since arriving in Hanoi, navy lieutenant Porter Halyburton had followed the Code of Conduct and remained uncooperative. Each time he had refused a request, the Camp Authority promised worse punishment. Each time he duly received it. Life grew harder and harder for this North Carolina native. Finally, prison officials warned that continued refusal would send him to the *very* worst place. Undeterred, Halyburton again refused to cooperate.

Guards had dragged him to a new cell, opened the door, and pushed him inside. There, he found Fred Cherry, an injured black air force major. The Camp Authority apparently thought Halyburton, a young navy lieutenant from the South, would find caring for a wounded black officer who outranked him utterly intolerable.

"I didn't care that Fred was injured, black, or that he outranked me," Halyburton told Jerry. "I just didn't want to be stuck with an Air Force guy!" The punch line brought a laugh. Over the coming weeks, Jerry learned how Halyburton nursed Fred Cherry back to health. Their story inspired everyone in the Pool Hall. Sadly, inspiration usually proved fleeting in the camp. Day-to-day reality inevitably returned, and men once again confronted their fate of enduring long hours locked away in North Vietnam.

One day, Halyburton challenged Jerry to a chess match. *How the hell are we going to play chess*, Jerry wondered. The young lieutenant conveyed a plan that involved toilet paper, cigarettes, and bread. In their separate cells, the two men folded sheets of brown toilet paper so the resulting creases created a gameboard with sixty-four squares. They used cigarette butts to blacken every other square. Jerry and Halyburton then began saving bits of bread, which they molded into the requisite pieces; rooks, pawns, knights, and bishops all had their own distinct shapes. Once they'd assembled their pieces, they tapped their moves to each other through the wall. If Jerry sent "QKR5," he was telling his opponent he'd moved his queen to the fifth square in the column corresponding to his king-side rook. Halyburton made note and moved "Jerry's" piece on his board. Then he responded. So their games went for several days until both POWs had to eat their game pieces to avoid being found out during a cell shakedown.

By April of 1966, Jerry knew of nearly one hundred Americans who'd been shot down. He estimated more than half were in the Zoo. He kept a running list on a piece of toilet paper and recited the names alphabetically several times a day, impressing each one into his memory. As a senior officer, he wanted to know his men. He also wanted to know who'd arrived in Hanoi alive. If an American perished in prison, he would hold North Vietnam accountable.

Jerry had noticed that more POWs seemed to have cellmates, although he himself remained in solitary for the ninth straight month. Empty rooms, which hampered down-the-line communication, became rare as more downed American airmen crowded into Hanoi's camps. At least one other POW was usually on the other side of Jerry's wall, ready to whisper or tap.

A sly new North Vietnamese commander arrived at the Zoo that April. POWs nicknamed him "Fox" as he began clamping down on the American communication network. Fox knew POWs needed communication like an army needs intelligence or supplies, or like a man needs water. If he could outsmart the prisoners and crush the communication system, he could destroy the resistance. And if he eliminated the resistance, he could fulfill his orders to deliver propaganda and intelligence. After all, Fox had a job to do. Jerry certainly understood this. He knew war often boiled down to young men from different countries with contrasting orders doing their jobs to see *their* orders fulfilled. As commanding officers, Jerry and Fox would understand each other. But that did not mean Jerry would help his North Vietnamese counterpart in the least.

Soon after Fox arrived, workmen arrived in the Pool Hall, where Jerry resided. He watched them unhinge his louvered door and replace it with a heavy wooden one. Later, a work detail arrived to place heavy mats over his window. He watched helplessly as these men suddenly made communication extremely difficult. The grid-based tap code became more important than ever. While tapping seemed tedious—and it was—the POWs had nothing but time. Communication continued despite Fox's efforts and threats.

As commanding officer, Jerry became a clearinghouse of information. Taps sent information bit by bit to his cell. When he had sufficient information, he'd pass along a longer message to a neighboring POW who would whisper-shout messages to neighboring cellblocks. *Thank God for men with guts like that*, Jerry thought. Otherwise his little Pool Hall might be an island. Once messages made the leap to other cellblocks, someone would eventually carry the relevant messages to other prisons in the system.

Mostly, the information was routine. One day, Jerry tapped out, "GM LGUZ 12IN PS ALRDY HIT F BIO X 5 NOW GETG THRTS F BIO X PB LTR FM HOME X LLFOX IS NEW XO X NEW NAME LCDR RENDER CRAYTON NO OTH INFO X PB BP Q W SPOT SOS."

When the POW in the next cell received the coded information Jerry passed, he translated the taps: "Good morning. Larry Guarino says 12 men in the Pigsty have already been tortured for biographies. Five men are now being threatened with torture if they don't write bios. Phil Butler got a letter from home. Looks like Fox is the new executive officer of the camp. A new validated prisoner name is Lieutenant Commander Render Crayton. We have no other information on him. Phil Butler and Bob Peel had quizzes with Spot—same old stuff."

Another time, Jerry received "JD PS NEED CLRTY. Y OR N ON BIO." The men in the Pigsty needed clarity on Jerry's orders regarding writing bios. His order was no. Stick to the Code until the pain seriously endangered mind or body.

Since POWs did not have books to read or paper for drawing or mathematics, the complexity of the tap code kept their minds sharp. For Jerry to send a message, he had to track each letter he sent and know appropriate abbreviations. Likewise, recipients had to track letters, then discern numbers, words, and abbreviations from long strings of uninterrupted code.

Jerry often used taps to reinforce his orders against writing or cooperating in any way without taking torture. Interrogations continued under Fox's regime, and he wanted his men to maintain a united front. Fortunately, quizzes remained routine and torture seemed to subside for the time being. When Jerry arrived for a typical quiz, Fox asked, "How are you?"

"I am terrible," Jerry replied. "I want the rights provided by the Geneva Convention. I need medical attention for my festering wounds. I want to associate with my fellow prisoners. I want time outside to exercise . . ."

"Shut mouth!" Fox exclaimed. "You are not prisoner of war! You are criminal! If you want better treatment, you must show good attitude. You show good attitude, you will get better treatment. If you are reasonable, you get roommate. In meantime, we treat you like criminal.

"Did you know that this week, the People's Air Defense Forces shot down on the spot twenty-nine American aggressor aircraft? Do you know our people will never give up? Now I want you to write something. Here is pen and ink and paper. Write names of some of your squadron mates."

Predictably, Jerry answered, "I will not write."

Fox screamed, "You will write! If you do not write you will be punish!" Shaking a stack of papers, he said, "Here, here are writings from many of your fellows who have good attitude."

His enticement didn't work. "If anyone wrote, I know you forced him to write," Jerry said, "and . . ."

"Shut mouth," Fox interrupted. "Go back to your room and think deeply about your crimes. Think about how you get better treatment if you change your attitude."

Back in his cell, Jerry summarized the quiz for his neighbors, tapping, "Q W FOX SOS." *Quiz with Fox. Same old stuff.*

Chapter 4

PIGEYE

FOX FINALLY TIRED OF JERRY'S refusal to cooperate and his continued agitation. On April 20, 1966, Fox ordered him back to Hỏa Lò Prison for punishment. Guards sent him to retrieve his mat before leaving and he frantically informed his Pool Hall neighbors about his coming move. He downed the remaining water in his jug, fearing the Camp Authority might restrict his diet as part of his punishment. Less than thirty minutes later, Jerry was blindfolded and bumping along the streets of Hanoi. He heard the vehicle's engine cut back. He felt it turn slowly. He sensed walls around him. He smelled the Hanoi Hilton.

A guard removed his blindfold. He stared into a new face. It belonged to a short, muscular enlisted man in his thirties. He had angular features with high cheekbones and a thin mouth that struck Jerry as particularly cruel. His eyes bored into the American's. He exuded quiet confidence and radiated compressed strength, which completely unsettled Jerry. With his hand wrapped tightly around Jerry's thin arm, the man led Jerry through the Hilton's passageways. He took him to the room from which Bob Shumaker had encouraged Jerry to "go fishing" during his first weeks as a POW. The man pushed Jerry through the door.

Shumaker was gone. The room stood empty except for a desk and four stools. Globs of plaster covered the wall; Jerry wasn't sure of their purpose. He stood by as the new guard picked up one stool and placed it in the room's center, beneath a burning light bulb. The guard stacked another stool atop the first. He then placed Jerry on top of the tower, helping him balance there, four feet above the hard concrete floor. Jerry gained his balance and the man cuffed Jerry's arms behind him. The guard assessed his work, then left Jerry alone. The man had never uttered a word.

Jerry sat there, precariously balanced on the stool. He suspected that the Camp Authority planned to coerce him to write a letter of some sort. He wondered how long they expected him to hold out. Well, he'd last longer than they'd think possible, he resolved. And he'd *never* sign a false confession.

He stared ahead. He stared at the floor. He blinked at the single bulb. He stared ahead again. Nothing in the room changed. No noise penetrated the heavy door and thick plaster. His own coughs, sniffs, and grunts were the only sounds. Otherwise, quiet pervaded. Hours passed. Nothing changed. Occasionally, a peephole in the door opened quietly and shut quickly. Nobody ever entered.

Eventually, Jerry's bladder made itself known. With no alternative, he delicately dismounted the stools. He landed on his feet even though his hands were still cuffed behind him and useless for balance. The stools collapsed behind him. He walked to the door and used his nose to open the peephole. Then he kicked a stool along until it stood below the peephole. He shimmied his pajama bottoms down sufficiently, stood on the stool, and urinated through the open hole. Relief radiated through him. He felt a tiny sense of victory.

Unable to reassemble the tower of stools, Jerry tried to stage an accident. He scattered the stools on the floor. He scraped his cheek along the rough plaster wall and placed himself amid the collapsed stools. The next guard to slide open the peephole would think he'd fallen asleep and toppled over—if they didn't notice the puddle outside the door.

In time, the same guard peeked in. If he noticed the puddle, he didn't acknowledge it. He simply entered and efficiently reassembled the rig. He placed Jerry back on top and left. He brought no food or water. Nor did anyone else.

The second night Jerry heard singing. Then screaming and taunting. He looked to his right and saw angels on the walls, playing harps and forming a beautiful chorus. On his other side, the globs of plaster transformed into noisy devils. The angelic melodies from one wall battled a satanic ruckus from the other. The cacophony inside the room became unbearable, and Jerry felt his mind slipping away once again. He desperately clawed back his sanity and the voices faded. The angels and demons became plaster once again. Damn his captors for making him crazy, he thought. He screwed up his resolve: He would die before signing a confession. Then his mind began slipping once again. Angels and devils battled; the cycle never seemed to stop. As the second night became the third day, he'd still received no food or water. Dying seemed more and more likely.

During the third day, the peephole slid open and closed routinely. Jerry assumed the same guard was always watching him. Later that day, a new figure appeared. A young officer, perhaps twenty-five years old, entered in a formal uniform. He didn't introduce himself, but Jerry marked him as a man with standing. Jerry noticed the officer's large ears; he decided to nickname him "Rabbit."

The new officer began decrying the severe punishment meted out to Jerry. He promised he'd asked his superiors to try different methods, but with no success. Jerry decided higher-ups had sent young Rabbit to play the good cop in this game. He wouldn't have it. He told Rabbit he would not write a confession. He wouldn't sign away his honor—the only thing he had left.

"But I tell you man to man, Denton," Rabbit almost implored, "they are going to torture you tomorrow if you do not write a confession. I know you will not give in to

Rabbit, the Camp Authority's lead interrogator.

67

starvation. I have told them that. They will hurt you very badly. Maybe they will kill you."

"I won't write anything," responded Jerry. He also noted that Rabbit used the word *torture*. Until then, Jerry had never heard a North Vietnamese utter the word. Americans were *punished*, not tortured. *Beaten*, not tortured. *Starved*, but not tortured. He looked at Rabbit with disdain.

"Denton, my government will probably not even use the confession," Rabbit reasoned. "Maybe no one will ever read it." He might have been sincere, Jerry allowed, but it didn't matter. He said nothing. Rabbit continued, "My government knows that it is humiliating for you to write a confession, even if the confession is forced, and not credible. They hope the suffering will cause you to act more reasonable, but they will probably not publicize your confession. You have everything to gain and nothing to lose if you write. Your treatment will greatly improve, you will even get a roommate. Aren't you lonely after ten months alone?"

Yes, Jerry thought, *I'm losing my mind in solitary*. He was desperately lonely. He'd not seen an American face since his shootdown. His longest conversations had been with interrogators. He'd heard nothing from Jane. He'd written to her only once, and he had no assurance the Camp Authority ever mailed the letter or if she knew he'd survived.

He was an exceptional aviator. He belonged in a cockpit. How had he ended up fighting the war from a prison cell? But he suffered these abuses for the sake of his honor and his own orders. He would not cashier that sacrifice. Months ago, he had decided not to write again on point of principle. He would neither second-guess that decision nor compromise. He just stared at Rabbit.

The young officer searched Jerry's eyes. "We know we cannot break you by food or water," he said. "Tomorrow we get serious. Tomorrow we torture you." Jerry wondered what tomorrow would bring but said nothing. Rabbit must have wondered why this helpless old man—Jerry was at least fifteen years older than Rabbit—acted so stubbornly. With some resignation, he said, "We will allow you to rest some time tonight. You have until morning to change your mind." Rabbit turned and left.

The silent guard returned for Jerry. He took him off the stools and led him away from that terrible room where he'd dwelled without food, water, or comfort for three days. The guard took him to New Guy Village, where he'd begun his imprisonment the previous July. Once there, the guard uncuffed Jerry's hands from their position behind his back. He immediately stuck them into a set of stocks. The stocks were at such a height that Jerry could neither fully stand nor completely kneel. He remained in a maddening limbo for two hours, his arms extended, wrists locked in the stocks, and legs bent.

Rabbit came with crackers and tea. He unlocked Jerry, gave him the food, and suggested he eat and sleep. Instead, when Rabbit left, Jerry called softly out the window. His voice echoed along the space between the cellblock and the outer wall, as it had when he and Larry Guarino communicated during his first weeks of imprisonment. He called again. The voice of his Naval Academy classmate Jim Stockdale came floating softly back.

Stockdale, a notably philosophical aviator, slightly outranked Jerry and led the Americans in Hanoi, when he was not in isolation. Like Jerry, Stockdale had taken North Vietnam's worst treatment on numerous occasions and always emerged with his inner resolve unbroken. Stockdale's reserved stoicism contrasted to Denton's aggressive gung-ho style, but the two made an effective pair. Jerry was thankful they had finally made contact.

Jerry figured he'd already been condemned to the worst punishment the Camp Authority could muster, so he didn't care about being caught communicating. He spoke openly and briefed Stockdale on activities at the Zoo; he described his three nights atop the stools. Stockdale recognized the silent guard as "Pigeye." He reported that the Camp Authority had unleashed Pigeye in November 1965. He'd since become a universally dreaded presence in the Hilton; seeing him usually meant pain. Jerry learned that Pigeye had broken most Americans of any seniority and was an accomplished practitioner of medieval techniques. Using ropes and straps, he'd broken Stockdale more than once already. The salty commander didn't have much hope that Jerry could resist Pigeye's inducements.

Jerry aimed to die rather than submit; "I'm going in there to die," he told Stockdale, with cavalier flourish. Jerry riled himself up and imagined himself on a religious crusade. He told Stockdale that God might well consider him a martyr. He entrusted his old classmate with a message to carry home to Jane.

"Tell Jane I love her," Jerry implored, "but that I want her to remarry." Jerry was specific and unrelenting on this point and eventually obtained Stockdale's agreement. Secure in the knowledge that Jane would move on, he settled down. He believed this would be his last night alive and spent the hours reflecting on his rich life. He had done his duty through the years. Tomorrow, he'd do it one final time.

———

When Jerry's cell door opened the next morning, Pigeye walked in. In rough English, he asked if Jerry had changed his mind. Jerry had not. He would not write a confession of any sort. Pigeye showed no reaction other than to grip Jerry and walk him to Room Eighteen, the room where he'd undergone his first interrogation last July. Pigeye shut the door. Another guard cuffed Jerry's hands behind his back. The two men began pummeling Jerry's face and body with fists. He tried to act stoically and resist the blows, but soon he fell to the floor. The guards picked him up and resumed their beating until he fell down again. They spun him around the room; he banged into one wall after another, leaving streaks of red blood on the white plaster. Each time a blow landed, Jerry felt pain, then anger, then resolve. Was that all they had? This, he could endure.

Pigeye finally stopped the beating. He repositioned Jerry on the floor. The two guards used rope to lace up Jerry's upper arms, which were still cuffed behind his back. They dug their feet into Jerry's spine as they pulled the rope tight and drew his upper arms together. Rope pulled tight against muscle and bone. His lower arms lost circulation. Pigeye continued pulling Jerry's upper arms together until his elbows nearly touched. He felt one more cinch would crack his sternum in two and pull both shoulders from their sockets. He screamed with pain. Then Pigeye released the ropes and blood flooded back into Jerry's hands, unleashing blinding pain, an agonizingly intense pins-and-needles sensation that nearly made Jerry pass out. But his mouth stayed shut.

Pigeye tightened the ropes again. Someone lifted Jerry's cuffed hands skyward behind his back. Hands forced his head toward his toes. His hamstrings erupted in pain, as did his shoulders and spine. He became a ball of agony. Jerry could not stop himself from crying. He pretended to pass out, hoping that would make Pigeye stop, but the man just lifted up Jerry's eyelids and grinned. The torture continued. Soon, Jerry had only one thought: *How can I stop the pain?* The thought consumed him; the desire to end the pain overrode his every other thought and instinct. He knew there was only one way to escape. Desperately he whispered, Báo cáo, báo cáo, the Vietnamese term for "I submit." Jerry had broken. The room went black.

Chapter 5

THE INTERVIEW

JERRY SENSED COLD WATER trickling down his body as he slowly regained consciousness. He felt it swirl around his legs. His eyes registered dark walls; his ears registered only soft sounds of water. Beneath him, the floor was hard, cold, and grimy. He was naked. Someone held up his torso. Jerry opened his eyes and saw Pigeye watching him. As his eyes adjusted to the dim room, he saw his blood mix with water as it flowed down a drain.

"Wash," Pigeye commanded. He and the other guard left Jerry to himself. The trickle of water coming from the shower and the soft gurgle of the drain made the only noise. In the dim solitude, Jerry collected himself. Then he heard an American voice.

"Hey, ol' buddy," said a voice under the door. "What's your name?"

He tried to respond, but the shower drowned out his terribly weak voice. With tremendous effort, he rose to his knees and used his elbow to turn off the shower. "I'm Denton," he said, using much of his remaining strength.

The voice asked, "Jeremiah Denton?"

"Yes."

"God bless you, Jeremiah Denton. You did a wonderful job at the Zoo."

"I'm not doing a very good job now," Jerry replied.

"You're only human," the voice said. Then the voice told Jerry he'd arrived in Heartbreak Hotel, a section of seven cells and one shower in the center of the Hanoi Hilton. The voice identified itself as that of Robbie Risner, lieutenant colonel, US Air Force. Jerry knew the senior-most POW had been isolated somewhere in the system for months; many suspected he was at the Hilton, but nobody knew for sure. Risner had once commanded all the POWs, but the Camp Authority had silenced him. Jim Stockdale and Jerry had stepped into his place, but now Jerry, like Stockdale, seemed condemned to the same isolation in Heartbreak Hotel. Jerry surmised the Camp Authority aimed to decapitate the American leadership.

The men talked for some time before Pigeye returned and stopped the conversation. He took Jerry to Room Eighteen, where Jerry met an officer he'd not previously seen. The man's features, including his protruding ears, matched the description of an officer nicknamed "Mickey Mouse," who'd reputedly been haranguing other POWs. Mickey Mouse sat behind a desk. Pigeye placed Jerry on a stool, but he fell off. Pigeye propped Jerry up against a wall. Mickey Mouse asked, "Now Denton, you are ready to write a confession of your crimes against the Vietnamese people—and make a tape recording of it?" Jerry nodded. Mickey Mouse placed a pen in Jerry's hand. His hand was so gnarled from his torture session, he couldn't hold it. Mickey Mouse violently popped Jerry's fingers back into joint and dictated: "heinous crimes . . . Yankee imperialists . . . aggressors." Jerry bent over a notebook and tried to write. Then Mickey Mouse made him recite the same diatribe into a tape recorder. Torture had so addled his mind, he couldn't even speak. His tormentors gave him a reprieve; he immediately fell asleep.

They came at him again the next morning. When they handed him a notebook, he saw what he'd written the previous day. He'd attempted to write real words; he'd produced only pathetic spirals. Now, holding the pen like a dagger, he wrote a more legible confession. Pigeye poured hot coffee down Jerry's throat and he managed to recite the words aloud for the tape recorder. He described "vicious, revolting crimes [against] the innocent people and civilian buildings of the Democratic Republic of Viet Nam." He heralded "the brave and determined workers of an antiaircraft battery [who] shot down my aircraft" and "the kindness of heart of the Vietnamese government and people." Each word sickened him. He knew North Vietnam would broadcast the statement. He'd violated every point of Article V. What would his men think? What would his wife, Jane, think?

The Camp Authority let Jerry recover in New Guy Village. As soon as Mickey Mouse judged him well enough, he began receiving painfully long personal lectures about the history of North Vietnam. Mickey Mouse fervently espoused his country's perspective. Hồ Chí Minh had won Vietnam's independence from France, he reminded Jerry. Now, the revered chairman wanted a unified Vietnam as Western powers had promised in the treaty ending the French Indochina War in 1954. Now, the unpopular autocratic regime in South Vietnam, supported by the United States, might as well have been a foreign power. The people of Vietnam, North and South, wanted unity and, at long last, peace. The struggle was about independence and unity, not political ideology.

Jerry wasn't buying this version of history. But since his captors held the cards, Jerry held his tongue. The lectures lasted for three nights. Jerry wondered about the purpose. Were they preparing him for something?

In early May, shortly after finishing his nightly lectures from Mickey Mouse, Jerry met a handsome North Vietnamese officer. Jerry estimated him to be in his mid-forties, just slightly older than himself. His uniform fit his slender frame well, and he spoke English with a slight French accent. He informed Jerry that he ran the prison system in North Vietnam. He claimed that he'd been a captive of the French in this very prison. Jim Stockdale had told Jerry about the smooth major nicknamed "Cat." Apparently, Cat and his henchman Pigeye had worked over Stockdale and numerous other Americans. Torture didn't seem to be on Cat's mind this day, however. He wanted Jerry's cooperation.

"Denton," Cat said, "you are going to meet with some members of the press. Use your head, Denton. This interview is very important. Be polite and do what you are told. Remember what punishment you have received in the past. I need not say more."

"I'll be polite but that's all," Jerry said gruffly.

Cat, the North Vietnamese major who led the Camp Authority, gives orders to an American POW.

Cat sent Jerry back to New Guy Village. There, he tried to steel himself for more torture, but he feared his weakened body couldn't handle a single punch. Jerry found Robbie Risner had taken Jim Stockdale's place in the cellblock. He asked the senior air force officer for advice. Risner counseled that taking more torture would likely serve no purpose. He suggested Jerry meet the journalists and neutralize the interview.

"I'll go," Jerry replied, "and blow it wide open."

Robbie and Jerry prayed together before they each fell asleep.

———

The next morning, Pigeye roused Jerry and motioned for him to change from his red-and-pink pajamas into an austere gray outfit.

77

Pigeye made sure Jerry buttoned the shirt to the collar. Jerry slipped on his flip-flops, and Pigeye led him into the courtyard and placed him in a waiting jeep. A guard tightened a blindfold around Jerry's head. The jeep rolled forward. He heard it pass through the prison gate and felt it turn left onto the street.

Were he driving through Virginia Beach, Jerry would have heard the ever-present din of modern buses, cars, and trucks. As he rode through downtown Hanoi, he heard few other engines. Instead, clear voices, the soft tread of feet, and the subtle crunch of bicycle tires predominated. The sounds were an unwelcome reminder that he languished in a colonial prison in a town where rickety bicycles outnumbered cars. A year ago, almost to the day, he'd said goodbye to his family as USS *Independence* left Norfolk, Virginia, for the South China Sea. He'd been trapped in Hanoi for 328 days now. Jerry was confounded. *Why hadn't America rescued him yet?*

After driving approximately one mile, the jeep turned onto a noticeably quieter street and slowed. When it squeaked to a stop, Pigeye removed Jerry's blindfold and ushered him toward what looked like a clubhouse. His downcast eyes watched his flip-flops cross the porch and step onto inlaid floors and fine rugs inside the building. Pigeye stuck Jerry in a powder room and handed him a beer. Jerry desperately wanted the drink, but he needed all his wits. He poured out the beer. Wistfully, he watched the suds disappear into the drain.

As Jerry anxiously waited for his interview to begin, he recalled a conversation he, Jane, and his son Don had six years earlier, in 1960. They'd been reading a newspaper article about Francis Gary Powers, an American U-2 spy plane pilot downed and captured in the Soviet Union. At his public trial, Powers had pleaded for mercy. He confessed he was "a human being . . . who is deeply repentant and profoundly sorry for what he has done."

"Isn't it too bad that he wasn't able to stand up and say something," Jane had mused, imagining how the pilot might have defied the Soviets in public.

"Mom," Don had responded, "don't you know that they can make you say anything?"

"Yes," Jane said, "but wouldn't it have been great if he had found the courage to say something?"

Now, Jerry faced the same test as Powers. He might face the same judgment from his family. Would he answer questions as instructed by his Communist captors or would he summon the courage to speak his mind, to uphold his honor, to defend his country?

Presently, Pigeye yanked him from the bathroom and ushered him through open French doors. He walked into a veritable sunrise. Glaring television lights shone into Jerry's eyes. He blinked. Suddenly, he knew exactly how he'd submarine the interview.

A Japanese journalist wearing a white shirt and thick glasses motioned to an empty stool placed before a microphone; Jerry took a seat. The journalist asked Jerry to smile. Jerry just stared at him blankly. Jerry spied Cat and Rabbit seated behind the journalist alongside other North Vietnamese officers. They watched him intently, expecting him to toe their line, to answer as he'd been coached. Jerry knew they thought that surely, after weeks of indoctrination and punishment, he would cooperate.

With his moment so near, and his tormentors so close, Jerry's heart pounded inside his chest. He knew the price he would pay for speaking his mind. As he waited for his chance to dash Cat's plans for the interview, his hands began to sweat and he clasped them together. The camera started filming. He began to blink, slowly and deliberately.

One long blink followed by three long blinks; Morse code for T and O.

"How are you treated," asked the reporter.

Jerry responded softly. "I get adequate food and adequate clothing and medical care when I require it," he said. That answer would please Cat and Rabbit, but Jerry would not parrot their rubbish for the entire interview.

He gave one short blink, a long blink, and another short blink: R. Then he sent one long blink: T.

The reporter asked, "Denton, what is your feeling toward your government's action?"

He sent the letter U with two short blinks followed by one long blink, then answered, "I don't know what is going on in the war now because the only sources I have access to are North Vietnam radio, magazines, and newspapers."

Straining to focus on his eyes and the journalist's questions, he blinked quickly, slowly, then quickly: R.

"What do you think about the so-called Vietnamese War?"

"I don't know what is happening," Jerry qualified, "but

whatever the position of my government is, I support it—fully. Whatever the position of my government is, I believe in it, yes sir. I am a member of that government and it is my job to support it and I will as long as I live."

He finished his message with one quick blink: E. Jerry had used Morse code to blink out a single desperate word:

T —

O ———

R .—.

T —

U ..—

R .—.

E .

TORTURE.

The smile disappeared from the reporter's face. Jerry saw the military officers stirring, sensing the interview had gone awry. He felt certain the North Vietnamese had not noticed the message he sent in Morse code; he figured they were far more concerned with his defiant answers. He knew retribution would come soon and be painful.

It did, and it was.

Jerry Denton secretly blinking out *torture* in Morse code during a televised interview, May 1966.

Chapter 6

PARADE

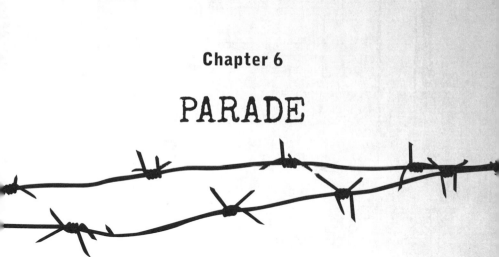

THE CAMP AUTHORITY sent Jerry Denton back to the Zoo on June 2, having extracted sufficient revenge for the off-script statements he made during his televised interview. Jerry felt quite certain Cat and Rabbit would never let him speak with another reporter. That was fine. For now, he needed to recover. The punishment had completely exhausted him. It left his hands so crippled he couldn't even wash his shirt when ordered; guards had to wash it for him.

When Jerry returned to the Zoo, so did summer. He'd nearly forgotten the oppressive Southeast Asian humidity he'd found in Hanoi when he arrived the previous July. Now he once again languished in the insufferable stock-still air of a solitary cell; no breath of wind could penetrate the concrete walls, wooden door, and thatched mats covering the windows. He lived in a tiny, dirty sauna. He was often too tired to communicate with his neighbors. He spent most of his days lying on a bamboo mat, unmoving, yet still soaked with perspiration. The small ration of water he received never quenched his constant thirst. He'd helplessly watch precious fluids ooze out of his body as sweat, making him even more thirsty.

For hours, he stared at the ceiling and the geckos that occasionally scurried across it. Sometimes, he'd lean against the wall and watch drops of sweat fall from his nose to the floor. For sport, he'd try to land them in the same spot. Each day was the same. Minutes passed like hours. Jerry continued to wonder how long his body and mind could survive.

———

Cat eventually broke the monotony when he launched his "Make Your Choice" program. The announcement came over the loudspeakers after he played confessions extracted from Robbie Risner and Jerry Denton. "Now, you have come to the place where you must make your choice," Cat told his prisoners. "You must decide whether you are going to take the good path, the path of Hồ Chí Minh and the Vietnamese people, the path of cooperation; or whether you are going to take the bad path, the path of resistance and death.

"Those who take the good path will receive good treatment. They will receive better food and lots of exercise and sunshine. They will have recreation. They will be allowed to read and study. When the time comes, they can expect to be released and go home to their families, perhaps even before the war ends.

"But we know that the vast majority will not be able to take the good path because they have been spoiled by the American system. They will understand the good path but will not be able to take it because they are set in their ways. We understand that, and they will be treated humanely."

Cat continued, "But also there will be a very small group of diehards. These people will take the bad path. They will refuse to admit their mistakes and will refuse to apologize and cooperate with the Vietnamese people. They will oppose us and resist us and lead others against us. That group will be severely punished. We are done with the diehard criminals.

"Now it is up to you. You must make your choice. Which way will you go?"

Jerry thought he fit quite nicely into the die-hard group; any path Cat and Rabbit considered bad, he considered good.

The North Vietnamese continued the propaganda offensive over the coming days. Cat and his officers repeated their promise to take cooperative POWs to "the good camp." There, they could roam outside, wear clean clothes, and enjoy good food. They could recover. Cat cajoled, "Forget your Code of Conduct. You may never go home. Make it easy on yourself. Make the good choice and cooperate."

Jerry Denton didn't believe a good camp or good food existed anywhere in North Vietnam. Furthermore, he could not let his men—his ragged, hungry, imprisoned little army—even think about softening their hard line. He would not let them stop dreaming of an honorable homecoming. The Camp Authority would have a fight on its hands. "We must all lie down in front of the train and slow it down," he sent down the cellblock. "We must do our best each time we are tested. That is the only way to defeat their aims." It was the only way for his men to survive mentally too. They needed a collective purpose to remind themselves they were still a unit of American fighting men. He reiterated that POWs should say nothing besides name, rank, service number, and date of birth. They should make no disloyal statements. The Code of Conduct was the only thing holding them together.

With increasing frequency, Cat summoned POWs into the Zoo's interrogation room. There, he would ask for intelligence, propaganda, and a final choice between the good and bad paths. Torture and threats pushed many POWs beyond the Big Four, but they rarely surrendered anything of value. In fact, the POWs spun so many lies in that room, they nicknamed it the Liar's Box. The POWs consistently made the wrong choice, at least from Cat's perspective. Their bravery made Jerry Denton immeasurably proud.

Jerry's men couldn't lie their way out of a confession, however. Pigeye soon appeared at the Zoo and plied his sadistic trade with alarming frequency. In response, Jerry ordered his men to die rather than give up classified information. Beyond that he ordered, "Take torture and before you lose your sanity, write something harmless and ludicrous."

The confessions extracted by Pigeye's ropes were always insincere, yet the coerced words were still devastating to morale when played over the camp's speaker system. Worse, every man feared his family and old squadron mates would hear the same recording. The groggy confessions would echo across the camp and through the cellblocks; pain was present in each word. Every time Jerry heard a confession, he knew an American had paid a stiff price for following his orders. He understood that nobody could hold out forever in the face of torture. He tapped out his counsel: "If you are broken, don't despair. Bounce back as soon as you can to the hard line." He inspired his men to do their best every time they faced Cat, Rabbit, and Pigeye. POWs had to remember they were soldiers, not criminals. Their actions and honor still mattered.

The English-speaking host of Radio Hanoi known as Hanoi Hannah often included the confessions in her thrice-daily broadcasts and chimed in to identify the confessor. Radio Hanoi broadcast throughout North and South Vietnam, delivering a mix of popular music, propaganda, news, and taunts; Hanoi Hannah became one of the war's best-known personalities. Americans in the South or at sea could turn off their radios, however. POWs could not. In her cheery, mocking voice, she reminded the American criminals, "You will be tried for your crimes. You will never go home."

When a confession from a newly arrived POW came over the Zoo's speakers one day, another POW tapped to Jerry in disgust: "God, I don't see how he could do that!"

"Don't condemn him," Jerry responded. "There is no telling what they did to him."

Later that week, the same POW admonished by Jerry

experienced Pigeye's ropes. He too read a confession. He returned to his cell and tapped to Jerry, "I am humiliated. What an arrogant fool I was to say what I did."

Jerry tapped back, "GBU." The three-letter acronym had become universally known and attained a meaning to POWs far deeper than the literal "God bless you." The letters conveyed a deep understanding of everyone's struggle. They offered forgiveness, solidarity, and encouragement. It was the closest expression to love that the POWs had.

The volume of orders coming from Jerry's cell and the resulting American resistance would lead the Camp Authority straight to the craggy, skinny POW from Alabama. Jerry knew the Camp Authority was especially galled by the POWs maintaining a command structure in direct defiance of all regulations. One day, Jerry heard Rabbit take to the PA system and announce, "Attention, all criminals. You know how die hard and obstinating Jeremiah Denton is. Well, we have succeeded in forcing him to confess his crimes. Those of you who remain obstinating will be forced into the same disgrace." Then he played the recording. Jerry recognized it as one extracted several months earlier; they were trying to undermine his leadership. Hanoi Hannah's happy voice added verification: "That was the voice of American war criminal Colonel Jeremiah Denton." *Commander* Denton seethed (the navy does not have the rank of colonel) until he received a touching note in the bathhouse from his men. Using toothpaste on toilet paper, the POWs had written, "We want to express our admiration for the man who is keeping his cool under this kind of pressure. We are proud to serve under your leadership."

The routine of boredom and isolation with occasional moments of interrogation and pain continued through June 1966. Routine at least made prison life predictable and relatively manageable. POWs generally found that change led to worse conditions. That summer they were right.

On June 29, 1966, a low rumble rolled through the summer air over Hanoi. It carried to the Zoo, where Jerry Denton heard it. For a moment, he mistook it for a summer thunderstorm. The rumble continued and he recognized the sound as bombing, not thunder. The POWs realized President Johnson had finally decided to bomb Hanoi itself. Never had US aircraft attacked Hanoi, and this new threat terrified the prison guards. It elated the Americans. Finally, planners had chosen a target of consequence, unlike the notably *in*consequential outposts across North Vietnam that US aircraft had attacked since the air campaign began. If North Vietnam's air defenses downed any American pilots on this day, at least the pilots would be flying a mission that mattered. The bombings of June 29 seemed to mark a turning point; America would bring the war to Hanoi. The POWs were certain North Vietnam would seek peace. Homecoming would surely come soon.

On July 6, Jerry noticed a change. Guards seemed tense and

activity at the Zoo increased. POWs began to speculate. Tapped messages flew up and down the cellblock as the men caught glimpses of other Americans outfitted in shirts with stenciled numbers on the back. Could this be preparation for a return home? Had the bombing convinced North Vietnam to negotiate? Jerry Denton's innate optimism filled him with hope, despite his efforts to temper it with the disappointing lessons of eleven months in prison. His imagination ran unchecked in his solitary cell. When he donned his own shirt with newly stenciled numbering, he could smell the ocean at Virginia Beach. He was going home.

Late that afternoon, guards opened Jerry's cell, blindfolded him, and pulled him into the hallway. They fastened his rubber sandals to his feet with gauze, then handcuffed his right hand to another prisoner's left. Guards herded the pair into a waiting truck, and they sternly ordered the POWs not to communicate. Beneath the tarp covering the truck's bed, Jerry found other Americans. Joy rushed into him like a storm-swollen river; he was no longer alone. He and everyone else immediately began to communicate. He pressed his knee against his neighbor's, to whom he'd been handcuffed. He tapped out, "D-E-N-T-O-N." The neighbor tapped his knee back: "P-E-E-L." Jerry sat next to air force lieutenant Bob Peel. Knees, toes, and fingers tapped silently but rapidly around the truck, and soon Jerry knew the roster of Americans with him. The truck's engine turned over, and it lurched into gear. Jerry heard another truck start nearby. They were in a convoy, and Jerry was sure they were airport bound.

They weren't.

The tide of optimism that had buoyed Jerry began to subside as he heard the noises of downtown Hanoi. The truck stopped at what seemed like the city's center, and guards began pulling the POWs from the backs of the trucks and removing their blindfolds. Jerry looked around and saw the old French-built Hanoi Opera House. The colonial landmark made the scene seem momentarily Parisian. A guard shoved Bob Peel and Jerry into the fifteenth row of a column of POWs twenty-five pairs long. Uniformed soldiers with fixed bayonets spaced the pairs eight feet apart. Apparently, they were to be marched through Hanoi.

The POWs never entirely lost their sense of humor, and one prisoner, anticipating what would come, sarcastically exclaimed, "A parade! Oh, boy, I love a parade!" The Americans snickered as guards shouted for silence.

Rabbit soon appeared, wearing a pressed uniform and armed with a megaphone. "You must remember that you are all criminals," he began. "Tonight you are being taken to your public interrogations so that all the world will know your terrible crimes . . . Today you will see the fury and hatred of the Vietnamese people. They will try to kill you. We cannot protect you. Show proper attitude for your crimes. If you repent, you will see our lenient and humane treatment. If not, the people will decide what to do with you."

Homecoming had clearly not arrived. Instead, the POWs were being paraded through Hanoi so the populace could vent anger stoked by the recent American bombings. Jerry could see crowds of citizens gathering along the roadside and standing on brightly lit bleachers. The men and women were boiling. They were angry. He knew they were hurt. He imagined they felt helpless as American warplanes soared distantly overhead and rained bombs on their city. The people below could only hope the bombs wouldn't land on them. Many had likely lost family and friends. They craved vengeance. The POWs were their nearest targets.

The march began as dusk became night. Floodlights quickly transformed night back into day, leaving the POWs no place to hide. Jerry spied several news cameras. He grinned and flashed a victory sign, extending his index and middle fingers in a V. After several moments, he retracted the index finger and rotated his left hand, middle finger still extended. He grinned as he shot the bird to the cameras.

As the guards prodded the Americans forward into the light, Rabbit ordered, "Bow your heads in shame for your crimes!" Guards used rifles and fists to make the prisoners comply. "Bow! Bow!" they shouted. Jerry knew images of the march would reach America, and he did not want his men looking guilty or defeated. "You are Americans!" he bellowed. "Keep your heads up!"

His order crackled like electricity along the twin columns. His men complied instantly, holding their heads high despite blows from the guards. The march advanced toward the grandstands, where Rabbit and other officers stoked the crowd and organized chants: "Down with the imperialist American aggressors! America get out!" The Americans walked slowly, some of them limping, through the valley created by the tall stands. Yells and

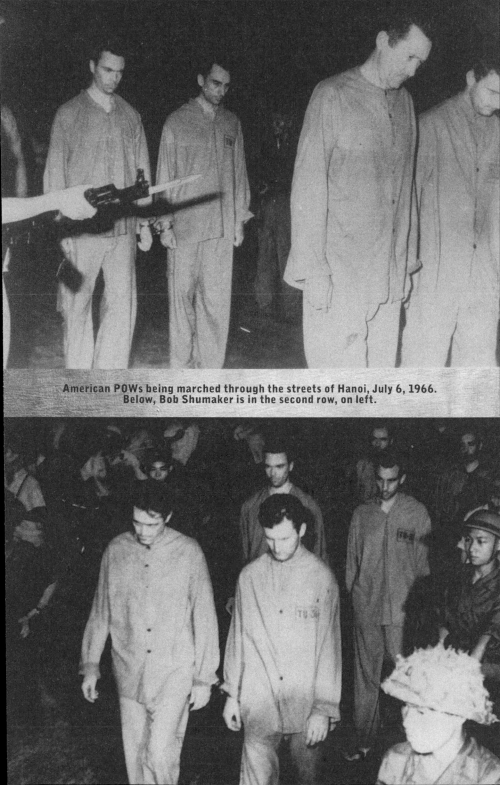

American POWs being marched through the streets of Hanoi, July 6, 1966. Below, Bob Shumaker is in the second row, on left.

chants cascaded down on top of them like a demoralizing avalanche. The scene reminded the Americans how far they were from home and the protection of the United States. They may have been marching together, but they were all alone.

One man mocked the downed pilots by shouting, "There, right before our eyes, is the 'might of American air power!'" The POWs, skinny and weakened from injuries and imprisonment, tried their best to soldier on.

A rock suddenly smacked the back of Jerry's head. He fell forward, pulling Bob Peel to the ground with him. Peel helped Jerry back to his feet. An instant later a man darted from the sidewalk and walloped Jerry in the groin. He almost fell over again. Up and down the line, Jerry could see objects flying from the sidewalks and battering the Americans. People began pushing through the cordon of guards surrounding the columns. They'd beat prisoners until guards threw them back into the crowd. The guards began to lose control; unexpectedly, they were no longer guarding POWs. Instead, they found themselves protecting the POWs and themselves from the inflamed citizenry of Hanoi.

Jerry felt another hard shot to the groin. As he crumpled to the ground in pain, he noticed the same man disappearing into the masses. Bob Peel again pulled Jerry to his feet. "He's not going to get me again," Jerry resolved to Bob. The next time the assailant came, Jerry and Bob used their conjoined right and left arms to deliver a well-coordinated punch that stopped him cold.

"If that son of a bitch comes out again, I'm going to kill him," Jerry yelled at a nearby guard, nicknamed "Spot." Spot knew Jerry was serious, and the next time the man tried for Jerry, Spot back-handed him and threw him into the crowd.

As he continued trudging through downtown Hanoi, Jerry spied an elderly woman weakly batting American pilots with her traditional straw hat. She wore an expression of weary anger. He noticed the tears in her eyes and wondered, *Who had she lost?*

The parade devolved into an outright melee as it neared the two-mile mark. Crowds left the sidewalks and pressed into the street, forcing guards and POWs through a narrow gauntlet. Beatings and projectiles had bloodied nearly every American; many men began to doubt they'd survive the night. Fears of dying in a Hỏa Lò Prison interrogation room took a back seat to fear of dying on a violent Hanoi street. Their destination and refuge seemed to be a looming stadium that Jerry spied as the march turned a corner. As the first POWs arrived, guards cracked open the stadium gates to let them through. Guards had to push the gates closed after each pair to keep out the surging mob.

By the time Jerry Denton and Bob Peel approached the stadium, they were alternately staggering and crawling forward through the angry crowds. They *had* to get to that stadium. They stood up and resolutely punched, kicked, and bulldozed their way through the final yards, using the very last of their energy. Guards pulled them through the gates to safety. Inside, Jerry and Bob Peel were unshackled. They were dog tired but safe. They had survived yet another trial. They stumbled to the stadium's track, where they joined other survivors. The march had exhausted guards and prisoners alike. They lay in separate groups, quietly talking about their harrowing night and enjoying a rare moment of peace. Many imprisoned Americans had not seen the night sky for months. Jerry looked up and wondered if Jane and their children might be seeing the same stars.

Chapter 7

BACK TO THE ZOO

WHEN JERRY RETURNED to the Zoo later that night, a guard removed the strips of gauze that had bound his sandals to his feet during the march. The rags were filthy. The guard used one to blindfold his prisoner. He stuffed the other into Jerry's mouth. It tasted of sweat and pavement. The guard marched Jerry along the grounds. He smelled Lake Fester, the stagnant swimming pool. It smelled fetid as always. Jerry could hear mosquitoes swarming above it. The guard pulled Jerry's arms behind his back and cuffed them around a tree. The guard left. The mosquitoes descended. Jerry had joined what the POWs sarcastically dubbed the Garden Party.

Jerry stood against the tree, his arms and back aching, cuts on his face and body still bleeding. He could taste the streets of Hanoi in his gag. Occasionally, a guard would saunter by to slug him. He finally managed to cough his initials in code: JD. From his left, he heard two coughs, then five: J. Then one cough followed by three: C. At least fellow naval aviator Jerry Coffee was there with him.

A guard released Jerry at daybreak and took him to see Fox, who still commanded the Zoo. Fox ordered the guard to wipe Jerry's dirty, bloody face. The guard complied carelessly. Fox sharply ordered him to do better, then sent the guard out of the room. Fox stunned Jerry by asking his thoughts on the previous night's march. No North Vietnamese official had ever asked his opinion about *anything*; Jerry did not waste his opportunity.

He erupted, "You fools! It's the biggest mistake you've made. Parading prisoners in the streets is a return to barbaric times. I have nothing but contempt for your utter cowardice. The spectacle of helpless prisoners being paraded through the streets will bring a wave of criticism from the world."

Jerry expected a fist or rifle butt to his face, but neither came. Fox asked if Jerry had finished. He had.

Fox said, "I have something to say to you and I request that you remember it for a long time. These words are important. Do you understand?"

Jerry nodded and Fox continued, "The march was not the idea of the Army of Vietnam. The march was the idea of the people."

Fox essentially told Jerry the army disagreed with the Communist Party's leadership. Never had Jerry heard a North Vietnamese official come so close to criticizing the government or apologizing for anything done to the POWs. Jerry stumbled back to his cell, still under guard. He considered how it was a soldier's lot to follow government orders. The conflict in Vietnam had made young Americans and North Vietnamese alike face that hard reality.

As Jerry fell asleep on his bamboo mat 8,446 miles from home, his mind weighed the challenges still at hand. Cat's grand "Make Your Choice" campaign would continue unabated and his men needed guidance. How should they uphold the Code of Conduct in the face of more torture and coercion? How long could they resist, and if they'd never return home, why did it matter?

Jerry had long hours to weigh that very question when Fox placed him in rear cuffs and leg stocks on July 20. He sat immobilized in his cell, unable to swat away hungry Southeast Asian mosquitoes. He learned the necessity of entering a trancelike state of reminiscence so he could transport his mind away from the dreadful present. He went back to McGill Institute, his high school in Mobile, Alabama, and his football coach Ed Overton.

Jerry recalled two things Overton had said. First, he always reminded his teams, "To be a champion, you have to pay the price every minute, day in and day out." Jerry wondered how many more minutes he'd have to pay the price in Hanoi. He'd paid it for 367 days already, 528,480 minutes.

He also recalled losing a key game during his senior year. Jerry played quarterback and gave every bit of his energy, mind, and body to the game. He lost a tooth, bloodied his nose, busted his mouth, and utterly exhausted himself. Still, McGill lost. Coach Overton spoke to the players after the game and singled out Jerry. He said, "Denton rose to the occasion. He has that in him. If all of you had played like he did, we would have won." The words embarrassed Jerry at the time, but they also stuck with him.

Now, thousands of miles and twenty-some years removed from McGill Institute, how could he inspire his men to fight like he did that night? Nobody measured the score in this contest with points; nobody recorded wins and losses in lights. But Coach Overton's lesson still applied. Jerry knew he had to set the standard. His duty was example.

He passed five days and nights locked in stocks. His muscles weakened daily, but he screwed up his mental strength. He guessed Fox was using the week's punishment to soften him up for a confession or biography. He guessed correctly. He refused Fox's request when it came on the fifth day. Fox promptly sent him to a Zoo cellblock known as the Gate. Guards dressed him in long sleeves and pants, locked him in rear cuffs, and roped his ankles together. They left him inside a veritable steam oven. The room had no ventilation. The July sun beat on the room all day. Sweat soaked Jerry's clothes. The wet clothing then caused boils to erupt. Mosquitoes bit into his exposed skin. He slept on a filthy concrete floor. He did learn to unlock his cuffs with a nail; he just had to listen closely for approaching guards so he could relock them before being caught.

After three weeks of slow-grinding punishment, Jerry still refused to write anything. Fox sent Jerry back to the tiny closet in the Auditorium. A guard nicknamed "Happy" used a rope to tie Jerry's arms behind his back. Then he left him in darkness. Jerry figured out how to loosen, then untie the ropes to afford himself some sleep at night. One night—at least he thought it was night—he heard boots approaching hurriedly. The door opened before he could retie the ropes. Happy noticed. He was livid. He knocked Jerry against the wall and retied his arms tighter than ever. Punishment continued the next day with two guards beating him around the cell and lifting him up by his arms, which were still tied behind him. Jerry marveled that his shoulders didn't pop. Finally, the pain grew too intense to resist. Beaten, he agreed to write a confession. At least it had taken three weeks to extract.

After Jerry inked the statement, Fox returned him to the general population in the Pool Hall. The inhabitants quickly reminded him how poorly they fared. One tapped to Jerry that POW Jim Mulligan looked like a prisoner at a Nazi concentration camp. He learned Jack Fellows couldn't use his arms, nor could Norlan Daughtrey. Ron Bliss had a major head injury. Nearly everyone was debilitated, yet the Camp Authority still put these men through the ropes and other means of torture. How long could POWs survive under these conditions? How could Jerry ask them to suffer even more?

Jerry had a two-week respite before the Camp Authority demanded he cease inciting other POWs to resist. Willing to endure torture again, Jerry refused. He would not quit his most important duty. A cadre of guards soon visited his cell and rigged a new coercion device. They sat Jerry on a pallet with his legs out straight. They cuffed his hands behind his back and placed his ankles in irons. A rope ran from the irons through a pulley and back to the pallet. By tightening the rope, guards could raise Jerry's outstretched legs. They began gradually. Every day, the rope was tightened and his legs lifted higher. The iron bar ate into his Achilles tendons. By and by, it broke the skin. His ankles swelled and oozed beneath the iron cuffs. His lower back ached more and more. After five days, Jerry noticed that the torture rig was affecting Happy, the guard assigned to Jerry. Happy would be weeping every time he left Jerry's cell.

On the tenth day, Jerry broke down. With tears in his eyes, he gave himself to God. He could take no more on his own. He'd reached yet another limit and sought peace in his last refuge.

"God, You've got it," he offered. "I can't take any more. You handle it, I'm putting it entirely in Your hands."

The instant he surrendered himself, he felt an extraordinary peace. It rooted deep inside him. He felt warm and comforted. The hurt vanished. He no longer felt alone.

When Happy ratcheted up Jerry's legs a short time later, blood trickled from his ankles. Yet Jerry did not feel pain. He looked calmly at Happy. His expression asked, "Why are you doing this to me?" The two men locked eyes. Happy dropped the rope and ran from the room. Jerry heard a shouting match outside. Happy returned and loosened the ropes. The next day, Happy took Jerry out of the punishment rig. He applied ointment to Jerry's ankles. Since Jerry could no longer walk, Happy and another guard half carried him to a room in another cellblock. Alone, he considered his ten-day ordeal. For the first time ever, they had not coerced a statement of any sort. He had finally won.

When the guards left, Jerry tapped, whispered, and even shouted, but he could raise nobody. The Camp Authority had isolated him again; Jerry was sure they wanted to prevent other POWs from learning he had beaten their game. He drew deeply upon that warm sense of pride and the power of his abiding faith. He hoped word of his example would somehow reach his men.

The Camp Authority never truly succeeded in isolating Jerry Denton. They eventually ended his exile, and he continued to lead his ragged fighting force at the Zoo in battle after losing battle with their adversaries. Somehow, he motivated broken men to rebound and willingly fight another round. They sacrificed for one another. At times, they collected extra rations for POWs in acute need. When the Camp Authority tried to starve a confession out of POW Bob Jeffrey, Jerry's neighbor Bob Purcell requested he be allowed to give part of his rations to Jeffrey. Jerry granted permission, although he wasn't sure how Purcell planned to accomplish his plan. A short time later, Jerry heard noise above his cell. A ceiling tile suddenly disappeared. In its place appeared Bob Purcell's face, wearing a wide grin. Jerry passed bread to Purcell, who scampered along the rafters to relieve Bob Jeffrey, stopping above other cells to gather extra rations. He used the afternoon siesta to run food and water to Jeffrey and other POWs in need at the Pool Hall.

Once, guards entered the cellblock during one of Purcell's excursions through the attic and began checking cells. The POWs raised a collective ruckus and banged items around their cells to cover Purcell's rapid retreat. He hurried along the rafters, dove through his ceiling, and crashed into his bunk. A guard opened his door moments later. Purcell said he'd fallen while exercising.

———

By January of 1967, Jerry had passed 554 days in North Vietnam since parachuting into the Mã River—and he'd never had a cellmate. If he'd had a choice between Pigeye's ropes and more loneliness in solitary confinement, Jerry might have picked the ropes. The depression of solitude grew worse each day. He found emotional torture just as brutal as the physical. Unexpectedly, the Camp Authority granted him relief on January 23, 1967.

Guards opened Jerry's cell door and motioned for him to gather his belongings. With no say in the matter, he complied. He'd become accustomed to trips into the unknown, and he really couldn't imagine how his situation could get worse. He trudged down the corridor.

Guards guided him to an office and sat him before an officer who fit the description of a new man POWs had nicknamed "Lump." Shortly, the door opened behind Jerry. He turned and locked eyes with Jim Mulligan. He'd known the gruff Irish Catholic with big sideburns from USS *Independence*. Jerry couldn't stop grinning.

"Hi, Jerry," Mulligan said, extending his hand.

"You know each other?" Lump asked.

"Yes," Mulligan answered. "We served together on the East Coast on board *Independence* some years ago."

"Good," Lump said. "Denton, how many aircraft do you have on the *Independence*?"

Jerry remained silent.

"How many aircraft does the *Enterprise* have, Mun?" he asked, calling Mulligan by his "Vietnamese" name and referencing the carrier to which he was most recently assigned.

"Normally about one hundred and fifty or so," Mulligan replied, roughly doubling the actual complement.

"Denton, you see the good attitude Mun shows by answering my question. You must learn yourself to be more cooperative. Since today the Camp Authority permit you to live together, you must not talk loudly and must obey the regulations of the camp.

"You may return to your cell with your friend," Lump said to Mulligan. Mulligan bowed and left. Jerry did the same. Jerry tried to hide his elation as he followed Mulligan toward their new cell. The Camp Authority had found perfect cellmates. Both were devout Catholics, and they had thirteen children between them.

"God, I'm glad to see you," Mulligan said when the guard had left them. "I've

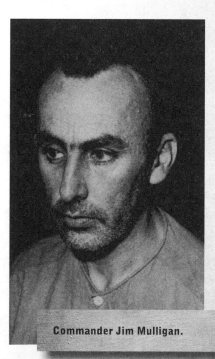

Commander Jim Mulligan.

105

been so lonesome that the past couple of weeks I thought I was losing my mind. You've been solo for eighteen months, twice as long as I have. I don't know how you kept your sanity."

"Jim, I prayed a lot and it helps more than anything else," Jerry answered.

Mulligan thought on that, then switched his attention to communication. "Watch for the guard and I'll pass the word to [Jerry] Coffee that you are with me," Mulligan said. Then he tapped, "JD MV IN W ME GOG WASH SOON CU AFTER CHOW. GBU." Jerry translated silently: "Jerry Denton moved in with me. Going to wash soon. See you after chow. God bless you."

At the washbasin, both men stripped down and looked at each other. They didn't say anything for several moments. Then Mulligan said, "Jerry, you look like one of those starving Jews in the German concentration camps."

Looking Mulligan up and down, Jerry replied, "Jim, I might look bad, but I don't look as bad as you do! You must weigh about ninety pounds. When you were first shot down I saw you in the yard at New Guy Village hanging out your clothes and you looked twice as big then as you do now. Are you eating everything they give you?"

"Hell yes," Mulligan answered. "I eat everything but I've had [diarrhea] since last summer. Every once in a while I pass a bucketful of worms. Last month I got rid of a tapeworm that was over three feet long. It scared the hell out of me."

The two POWs agreed they each looked terrible. Maybe a good wash would help. They dumped buckets of water over each other and began scrubbing. "How about washing the middle of my back," Jerry suggested. "I haven't been able to reach it and feel clean since I was shot down." Mulligan scoured Jerry's back with his washcloth; Jerry reciprocated. They finished bathing, washed their clothes in the wastewater, then enjoyed the morning sunshine until the guard herded them back inside their cellblock. They found breakfast waiting. They sat down to the first meal either had shared with another American since arriving in North Vietnam. Jerry said grace. Both men agreed that dining together made the stringy soup and rice seem like food from a feast. They felt human once again. They talked nonstop for two days.

Jerry had trouble absorbing all their conversation. His mind followed the person-to-person conversation sluggishly; he still felt the effects of torture and solitary. But he did his best and both men grew hoarse as they talked in whispers throughout the night.

Whenever Jerry's conversation drifted toward griping, Mulligan stopped him. He shared something his wife, Louise, had said: "If you didn't have a sense of humor, you should never have joined." Jerry took the words to heart.

On the third day, the guard Jerry knew as Happy opened the door and told Jerry to dress up and gather his belongings. Jerry had tears in his eyes as he shook Jim Mulligan's hand, not knowing when or if they'd see each other again. "God bless, Jim," Jerry said. "GBU," Mulligan replied.

The guard led him away but not toward another cell. Someone tied a blindfold around Jerry's eyes and put him in a truck. Soon, he began recognizing sounds of downtown Hanoi. He felt the truck slow and turn. He listened to the distinctive echo of a tunnel, sniffed the musty air, and knew he'd returned to Hỏa Lò. When the truck stopped, several hands pulled him out and led him across stone pavers; he felt the worn stones through his thin sandals. A door opened and closed. Another door opened. Someone pushed him inside a cell and removed his blindfold. Jerry saw fresh paint covering newly constructed wooden walls; bamboo mats blocked the window. A single wooden bunk awaited him.

During the evening, he heard more noise, shuffling of feet and barked orders. It seemed other POWs were arriving, but the constant presence of guards stopped them from communicating. The area eventually grew quiet. A pair of sandals flopped down the hallway and a door closed. Two thumps indicated "all clear"; there were other POWs there indeed. The wooden walls began clicking with taps: initials, names. Jerry noted the lineup: senior navy commanders Jim Stockdale, Harry Jenkins, Jim Mulligan, and Howie Rutledge, along with younger officers Sam Johnson, Bob Shumaker, Nels Tanner, George McKnight, Ron Storz, and George Coker. Were this a baseball dugout, Jerry would have been on an all-star team. He knew the men surrounding him were influential leaders or juniors who'd proven exceptionally maddening to the Camp Authority. They'd all earned a reputation among the POW population—and among the North Vietnamese staff too. Although still in solitary confinement, Jerry very much felt the presence of these stalwart brothers in resistance.

Chapter 8

LITTLE VEGAS

JERRY SURVEYED HIS NEW HOME the next morning when a guard escorted him to wash. Like a lunar explorer making first prints, Jerry walked into a landscape he'd never seen. He entered an open dirt courtyard. Other than two almond trees, little grew in the packed earth. He observed low yellow buildings with long, barred windows that arched under the overhanging terra-cotta tiled roof. A ten-stall bathhouse occupied the area's center; that's where his escort nudged him. Inside, he found a large metal basin fed by a feeble trickle from an iron pipe. With his thin washrag and sliver of soap, he cleaned himself as best he could.

The permanence of the area worried Jerry most. It looked like the Camp Authority had refurbished this section of Hỏa Lò for long-term residence. The Zoo had been a temporary, makeshift camp; this space seemed designed to hold American POWs for years and years. That dreadful prospect deflated Jerry entirely.

Within a few days, each cellblock had received a nickname. The names came tapping through the wall and Jerry matched names and buildings; most shared names with famous casinos. He and his fellow rabble were in Stardust, next to the Desert Inn, on the courtyard's east side. Cellblocks Riviera and Golden Nugget formed the southern and western borders. Thunderbird bordered the yard to the north. The latrine was called the Sands. Jerry sensed air force fliers familiar with Las Vegas's Nellis Air Force Base had heavily influenced the naming; Little Vegas became the section's collective nickname. Within several hours, the POWs had counted off fifty-four prisoners across the cellblocks.

The propaganda system came next. With a sense of resignation, POWs watched workmen wire speakers throughout Little Vegas. The POWs may have escaped the Zoo, but they would not escape Hanoi Hannah. By 1967, she had begun reporting civil unrest and opposition to the war in the United States, something that profoundly unsettled the POWs. In April, she reported civil rights leader Martin Luther King Jr. had spoken out against the war. Dr. King delivered a speech that decried the destruction the war visited upon the poor in Vietnam and in the United States alike. He called for America to stop the war.

"In order to atone for our sins and errors in Vietnam, we should take the initiative in bringing a halt to this tragic war," King said. "We must stop now. I speak as one who loves America, to the leaders of our own nation: The great initiative in this war is ours; the initiative to stop it must be ours."

King's protest added another US leader to the list Hannah reported had turned against the war. The POWs were left to wonder what had changed in America and what that meant for them.

In Hanoi, the POWs had no choice but to press the fight. The imprisoned army grew steadily, with new American shootdowns arriving regularly; frequent diatribes from Hanoi Hannah welcomed them. Jerry attributed the increase in prison population to heavier American bombing efforts. Perhaps, he mused, intensified bombing would drive North Vietnam to negotiate. Maybe homecoming would arrive soon. Jerry tapped his optimistic views to others. Few shared them.

Newer POWs had a difficult time applying the Code of Conduct to their specific situation in Hanoi. To help, Jim Stockdale, Jerry, and other leaders implemented a set of rules. They made the aspirational Code of Conduct into a tactical guide for actions in Hanoi. The acronym BACK US helped everyone remember:

BOW: Don't bow in public. Don't let the world see POWs showing deference to their captors.

AIR: Stay off the air. No prisoner should read or say anything into a microphone for broadcast or recording. If the Camp Authority applies duress, POWs should endure at least a week in irons or undergo some equivalent before submitting.

CRIMES: Admit no crimes. Americans are soldiers on a mission, not criminals. They need to remember that and not give the North Vietnamese statements that the public could misconstrue.

KISS: Don't kiss up or kiss them goodbye. POWs should neither curry favor nor demonstrate any gratitude at all. The Camp Authority treated POWs abysmally and POWs should not forget it. Nor should POWs kiss their captors goodbye, as the saying goes, at homecoming.

UNITY OVER SELF. Nothing is more important than supporting the man in the next cell. Accepting special favors or going maverick could undermine cohesion, which would weaken the POWs' collective position against the Camp Authority. The Americans must maintain a united front, regardless of immediate self-interest.

Several days after the initial BACK US rules were announced, Rabbit raised the ante. The young political officer's voice came ringing over the camp speakers. He said, "You are criminals. You must work for us. You must pay for your keep. You have obligations to the Democratic Republic of Vietnam. You must atone for your crimes and thereby enjoy the historic lenience and generosity of the Vietnamese people." He repeated the statement twice more.

Then Rabbit took aim at Jerry Denton, Jim Stockdale, and other American leaders. He warned, "A place is being prepared for those black criminals who persist in inciting the other criminals to oppose the Camp Authority. It is a dark place to which they will be banished. And those who repent, [who] show true repentance in actions as well as words, will be permitted to go home even before the war is over."

Damn Rabbit. He'd threatened Jerry and the POW leadership. He'd also aimed to split the POWs. Jerry knew that after up to three years in prison, some POWs would become susceptible to the Camp Authority's enticements. A cooperative few would wreck the POWs' collective unity. It would be every man for himself, all competing to win early release.

Within minutes of Rabbit's broadcast, Jerry heard taps. Stockdale had dubbed the Camp Authority's offer the "Fink Release Program," or FRP for short. If you leave early, you're a fink. He issued a related corollary to BACK US: "No early release. We all go home together."

Less than a week later, an additional corollary came tapping into Jerry's cell: "No repent, no repay. Do not work in town."

Jerry puzzled over the command. Then he heard Rabbit make a new announcement over the camp speakers. "Criminals will be given an opportunity to atone for their crimes in a meaningful way," Rabbit promised. "They will be allowed to help the Vietnamese people clean up the debris of bomb damage. Work parties are to start among volunteers and the work will afford you the opportunity of fresh air and exercise. A bath will be available to each volunteer after returning from the bomb-site area. You will be approached individually."

Now the new corollary made sense. Jerry encouraged his men to resist working in town. They would *not* give North Vietnam's propaganda doctors images of penitent criminals helping the enemy. Jerry reminded his men they were American officers, not common criminals. They would not work on a chain gang in Hanoi. During the next weeks, Cat and Rabbit asked nearly every American in Little Vegas to participate; not one said yes.

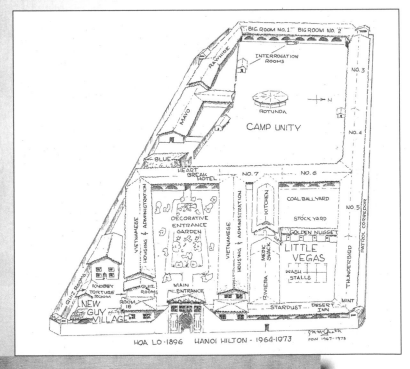

Map of Hỏa Lò Prison, also known as the Hanoi Hilton. Sketch by former POW Mike McGrath.

In May of 1967, Jerry found himself in the prison commandant's office with Jim Mulligan once again. An officer known as "Flea" for his small size and irritating nature said, "The camp is very crowded with American prisoners. The camp commander permits you to live together. You must obey the regulations of the camp and not communicate. My guard will take you to your new room."

Jerry bowed and said, "Thank you." He picked up his gear and followed the guard to Stardust cell 5.

The room was eight feet long and four and a half feet wide. Two bunks occupied most of the space. A typical bamboo mat covered the window, stifling any circulation. The cell felt like a steam room.

"I'll take the upper bunk, Jim," Jerry said, climbing up. "You'll never be able to climb up there with your bad arm."

Jerry rushed to erect the mosquito netting he'd been issued; Mulligan did the same. Outside the netting, the voracious little insects swarmed, awaiting their chance.

Once settled, the two former roommates resumed their conversation from January. They lay sweating in the stagnant air, talking quietly to avoid attracting guards. Mulligan related an interesting story that reminded Jerry that the Americans and North Vietnamese were ultimately both doing their jobs. As Mulligan finished a quiz that winter, an opposing officer had said, "You and I are military men. I do my job and you do yours.

I hope you will be with your family before too much longer. This war is a hardship on us all. Good luck to you."

By the next morning, Jerry could stand the heat no longer. He couldn't sleep, nor could he breathe. He yelled "Báo cáo!" to a passing guard, who soon returned with Flea. The Vietnamese phrase *báo cáo* could mean *I submit* or *to report*.

"Our room is too hot," Jerry stated. "We need to have the cover taken off the window." To Jerry's surprise, Flea agreed. Within ten minutes, guards removed the mat. Jerry and Jim looked out the barred window into the courtyard and felt the glorious breeze. Then they staged a small war, killing as many lingering mosquitoes as they could.

From the summer's many new arrivals, Jerry learned Operation Rolling Thunder had lasted more than twenty-five months since its start in March 1965. General William Westmoreland had 448,000 troops in South Vietnam fighting Communist guerrillas who would attack and then vanish into the countryside. The air campaign continued, yet the war seemed no closer to ending. More than 10,000 Americans had been killed in action; by Jim Mulligan's count, more than 350 had landed in North Vietnam's prison system. Perhaps more disturbing, new POWs corroborated Hanoi Hannah's reports that many Americans were turning against the war. Jerry found that particularly hard to accept, especially as he battled Communists each day. He wouldn't change his mind about the war. And if he were to change his mind, a gulag like Hỏa Lò was the last place he'd do it.

On June 28, Jerry began whispering back and forth with a neighboring POW, Hugh Stafford, their voices carrying from window to window. Stafford whispered that he shared a cell with Red McDaniel, a good friend of Jerry's from Virginia Beach.

Happy to be in contact with an old friend, although sad McDaniel had wound up in Hanoi, Jerry asked, "Does Red have any messages for me?"

The reply came back, "Your son is burning up the Little League again!"

Jerry forgot himself and nearly shouted, "Hot dog!"

"Jerry, get off the wall!" Mulligan half yelled and half whispered from the floor, where he'd been watching for guards. Jerry kept talking.

McDaniel asked if Jerry knew Jim Mulligan. "Hell yes. He's lying on the deck clearing under the door for me right now."

"Tell Jim his wife is in Virginia Beach and knows he is a POW. Father Gallagher says they are all praying for him aboard the *Enterprise*."

Mulligan yelled at Jerry again. He kept talking.

Mulligan sprang to his bunk just as a guard burst through the door. The irate guard pointed at Jerry and shouted, "You communicate!" He left hurriedly. Jerry saw trepidation on Mulligan's face. "Hell, Jim," he said, "I'll tell them you were asleep and I was comming on my own out the window."

Minutes later, Jerry sat in a quiz room facing off against a new officer who seemed to have taken a position of importance in the prison system. POWs had nicknamed him "Rat."

"We have caught you," Rat said. "Who were you communicating with?"

"No one," Jerry said. "I was just calling out my name. Mulligan warned me not to do it, but I did it anyway. He had nothing to do with it."

"You sure?" Rat asked.

"Yes, I'm sure."

Rat still pressed to know what Jerry had said. Jerry refused to disclose more, so Rat ordered guards to apply rear cuffs and leg irons. Rat then sent Jerry outside to the bathhouse. Guards left him kneeling in the hot midday sun; he felt heat reflected onto him from the barren ground and each surrounding building. As he baked in the courtyard, he closed his eyes against the heat and prayed the rosary.

Hours passed. The courtyard grew hotter; he felt a fever take root. His ankles and wrists swelled against their iron bonds. He desperately needed food and water. Gradually, however, heat, pain, thirst, and hunger faded from Jerry's mind. He thought it odd, but toilet paper replaced them as his most pressing concern. He'd reached his limit of dirtiness. Using the nearby latrine bucket—which he badly needed to do—without toilet paper seemed one disgrace too many. Acknowledging the triviality of his request, he bowed his head and asked the Lord for assistance.

Jerry opened his eyes and saw a large, fuzzy leaf drifting toward him. It landed nearby and he maneuvered his body to snatch it with his hands, which were still cuffed behind him. He shuffled on his knees to the bucket and put the leaf to use. In Jerry's mind, the Lord had delivered a substantial victory.

It proved a short-lived one. Jerry wilted just like one of the weeds scattered about the courtyard. A doctor arrived later that day and took him to the Riviera cellblock. There, he removed Jerry's irons and cuffs. Jerry felt relief until guards blindfolded him, reapplied rear cuffs, and sat him on a low stool. For several days, he remained on the stool, fighting for sleep and suffering from fever. Worst, he wasn't resisting to avoid signing a confession or revealing communication secrets. He faced plain vindictiveness.

Finally, the doctor interceded and ended the punishment. Jerry could scarcely remember guards hauling him across the courtyard to Thunderbird. Likewise, he was only vaguely aware of them removing his cuffs and clothes. He collapsed on the floor and once again engaged in a struggle to maintain coherence. He did a poor job. He routinely flailed at the wall in a state of semi-consciousness, beating out his initials in code with his fists. Neighboring POW Bob Peel finally responded with some exasperation, "Okay, okay, we know you're in there!"

On July 8, 1967, guards arrived and ordered Jerry to stand up. His punishment had now lasted five days. For how many more would it continue? The guards walked him back to Stardust. They opened the door to Stardust 5 and ushered him into the dark interior. Jerry's eyes adjusted and he saw his friend Jim

Mulligan. Mulligan seemed like a midsummer's Christmas present.

The Camp Authority still watched Jerry closely, even in his weakened state. He deduced guards were under orders to stifle his influence by shutting down communication to and from his cell. They proved maddeningly effective. Jim Mulligan and Jerry became ever more isolated, even amid so many Americans.

From the information that trickled into Jerry's cell, he discerned the Camp Authority was even more determined to crush the American resistance. They'd focused on its two nodes—Jerry Denton in Stardust and Jim Stockdale in Thunderbird. Pigeye or other guards put nearly every POW in Little Vegas through the ropes. They didn't want military intelligence, apologies, or propaganda statements. They wanted the unfortunate subjects to name Jeremiah Denton and Jim Stockdale. They wanted to know which lieutenants worked closest with these disrupters. They wanted to know how the resistance worked. They wanted evidence.

Jerry heard from many POWs that the summer of 1967 was the worst of their lives. Nobody would willingly give up their commanding officer, but many became afraid they'd die if they didn't. The torture proved unrelenting. Jerry observed that the Camp Authority oddly seemed to need proof that he was behind the resistance before coming after him. Why else wouldn't they have just sent him away already?

On August 8, a guard Jerry recognized as "Pimples" opened the peephole to Stardust 5. He motioned for Mulligan to come closer. Mulligan complied and Pimples spat in his face. Jerry watched Mulligan spit a glob of phlegm right back at Pimples. Jerry knew trouble was coming. "Jim, they'll be here in minutes; the comm purge must be on good," Jerry said. "Pimples didn't come here to do that; he was *sent* here." They both used the bucket while they weren't confined to irons or stocks. Sure enough, Flea soon appeared and had both inmates clamped into leg stocks. The Camp Authority aimed to stymie the POW communication system and they went after its central nerve.

"We'll be out in twenty-five days," predicted Jerry dourly. He was thinking about September 2, the day North Vietnam celebrated its initial independence from France. The occasion had brought clemency for POWs in past years.

"Oh, I don't think it'll be that long," Mulligan replied.

"Yep," Jerry said with an uncharacteristic lack of optimism, "it'll be that long."

Guards soon confiscated their mosquito nets. The two friends remained in the stocks day and night, constant prey for Hanoi's bugs. Jerry could feel his already weak muscles atrophying further. Guards at least allowed Mulligan out of their Stardust cell for several minutes each day to empty the one latrine bucket the two men shared; Jerry stayed locked onto his bunk. His legs could barely move. Flea and Rat seem to share responsibility for the Hilton that summer and allowed both men a weekly bath. At least they could talk to each other. Guards still yelled at them, demanding they keep quiet, but the POWs didn't care. *What more can they do to us?* Jerry reasoned.

Life was not comfortable. One night, Jerry awoke needing to urinate. The one bucket the men shared lay on the floor. If Jerry didn't find an option quickly, Jim Mulligan below would get a shower. Finally, Jerry said, "Jim, I have to piss so bad I can't stand it!" He heard Mulligan drink from his cup. "Use this," Mulligan said. He handed up his drinking cup. "It's the only thing I can reach. Besides, I don't want to get wet down here." Jerry took it and soon felt much better. His bunkmate stayed dry. The next morning, a guard unlocked Mulligan, who emptied the cup and bucket. Jerry had to stay put.

Jerry came to know Jim Mulligan even more intimately. With weeks of uninterrupted time together, Jerry shared his life's story and his innermost concerns. Mulligan did the same. They considered each other through the lens of their common Catholic faith, which also helped sustain them hour by hour. Jerry would pass vast blocks of time in prayer, reciting the rosary over and over. He tried to remain thankful; many other aviators had died at shootdown. Jim Mulligan and Jerry believed their ordeal had purpose; they couldn't let themselves think otherwise. Perhaps God intended them to emerge as better men. They made themselves open to those lessons: *They couldn't control their circumstance, but they could control how they responded.*

Immobilized on his bunk day and night, tormented by mosquitoes, and covered with perspiration, Jerry's mind drifted to various parts of his life. He often returned to his years at the Naval Academy in Annapolis, Maryland. He'd decided to attend during his sophomore year at McGill Institute. He saw the 1937 film *Navy Blue and Gold*, starring Jimmy Stewart and Lionel Barrymore. After that, he didn't want to go anywhere but Annapolis. He admitted to himself he loafed along in high school. He thought the challenge of becoming a naval officer would summon his very best. He applied for admission.

After long months of waiting, he earned an acceptance and arrived on the Yard, as the Naval Academy calls its campus, in 1943 with brimming confidence but little understanding of his new world. He made an unfortunate entrance. Jerry had been a high school quarterback and never lacked swagger. First year midshipmen, called plebes, weren't supposed to show *any* swagger, however. Jerry arrived in Annapolis with an empty stomach. Before registering, he sauntered into the dining hall, filled a plate, and sat at a table with several upperclassmen. Galled by the temerity of this plebe, one upperclassman began a personal campaign to drive Jerry out of the Brigade of Midshipmen, the student body. Throughout the fall, he had Jerry running drills in the rain, counting out endless push-ups, and reciting naval knowledge and trivia. Finally, Alan Shepard, who would become the first American in space, feared the relentless hazing would, in fact, run this promising young plebe out of the Academy. He finally told Jerry's tormentor to leave Midshipman Denton alone.

Thinking back to those miserable months, Jerry abruptly proclaimed out loud, "Jim, if this place gets any worse it will be almost as bad as my plebe year at the Naval Academy!" Both men burst into laughter. Guards yelled at them, but they kept laughing. They had companionship. They had a common enemy. And they had little to lose. Release and homecoming seemed ever more distant and even unlikely.

As Jerry had predicted, guards released him and Mulligan from the stocks on September 2, North Vietnam's Independence Day. They mercifully returned the precious mosquito netting too.

The Camp Authority did not extend mercy for long, or to many. Several weeks later, guards arrived and dragged Jerry through the adjacent cellblock—the Desert Inn—and into a dark corner of Little Vegas. He thought he'd arrived in the Mint, a special punishment section about which he'd heard. Guards pulled his hands behind his back and cuffed them. A blindfold went over his eyes and a gag went into his mouth. The guards pushed Jerry through one small door into a small anteroom. They opened yet another door and shoved him into a filthy cell; to Jerry, all the Hilton's cells looked alike now. Worse, they smelled and felt alike: pungent, steamy, and hopeless.

He continued to suffer for the BACK US directive; the united POWs were maintaining their hard line against the Camp Authority. Nearly every quiz Jerry had in September and October focused on the POW leadership and its resilient communication system. Cat, Rabbit, and their henchmen seemed to obsess over framing POW leaders and exposing the command structure. POWs thwarted them at every chance; many paid a stiff price to protect Jerry, Jim Stockdale, and other leaders. After pumping Jerry unsuccessfully for information in one session, Flea said with some resignation, "Denton, I think that no matter what we do, you will not tell us anything [about the POW organization]."

"That's right," Jerry responded boldly. Flea looked at Jerry for a long moment, then sighed. "Get up. Go back to your room," he said, waving his arm. Jerry sensed a change for the worse was coming.

Chapter 9

ALCATRAZ

THE CHANGE JERRY FEARED came on the night of October 25, 1967. He heard the distinctive light, quick footsteps of guards as they rushed into the Stardust cellblock. Keys rattled, padlocked doors creaked open, and curt orders echoed along the corridor. Jerry's closest friends, his fellow Stardust prisoners, began shuffling by his door; he tried to identify them by their walk. Then a guard arrived for him. He carried a blindfold and Jerry turned around in resignation. The guard tightened the cloth around Jerry's head, then led him into the hallway.

Jerry felt his way forward through Stardust, then sensed the autumn breeze circulating through the alleyway between the cellblock and the prison's outer wall. For a moment, he appreciated the refreshment of being outside. A hand pushed Jerry into a kneeling position. His shoulders rubbed against other POWs; soft nudges in code told him George Coker and Howie Rutledge were next to him. The POWs knelt together in the alleyway; they heard others arrive and join them. They listened not only to the sounds of movement but to the rare sound of an open sky at night.

Someone grabbed Jerry's ear and wrenched him to his feet. He and some number of other POWs were led down the alley and into the corridor at Hỏa Lò's entrance; he could hear voices echo off the arched ceiling. Arms and hands loaded him into a truck bed. He sat on piles of metal pipes, which pinched his legs with every bounce of the truck as it rumbled through the quiet night to God knew where.

In fact, the truck carried the POWs to a tiny prison on a small street behind the North Vietnamese Ministry of Defense, at 4 Phố Lý Nam Đế. (*Phố* means "road" in Vietnamese. *Phở* means "soup.") The French had built the small thirteen-cell gulag in the 1950s especially for dissidents, troublemakers, and political leaders who required more isolation than Hỏa Lò Prison could provide. The new prison on Lý Nam Đế had removed enemies of the French regime from the world. There, they could no longer spread their political ideas or incite other prisoners. There, they effectively vanished.

The Camp Authority had reopened this most forlorn outpost, hoping it could help restore their control over the US prisoners. They looked across the entire prison system and identified the eleven Americans most responsible for stoking resistance and ruining their plans to subjugate American POWs. On this night, they rounded them up and sent them away.

The truck carrying Jerry Denton stopped after a short ten-minute ride. A hand pulled him down from the truck bed and

The small white buildings at center are the cellblocks at 4 Phố Lý Nam Đế, the prison nicknamed Alcatraz.

guided him forward. He descended several steps and sensed he'd entered a compound. His guard pushed him against a wall and left. Still blindfolded, Jerry listened intently. He heard the voices of guards, the shuffle of feet, the whine of hinges, the rattle of keys, and the clink of cell doors being locked.

Finally, a guard ushered him down a bricked path. He sensed a long building on his left and open space on his right. When he'd traveled along the building for forty feet, the guard stopped him and turned him ninety degrees to the left. Another guard fastened leg irons around his ankles, then removed his blindfold. Jerry stood in a dark courtyard facing the last room in a long cellblock. A small open doorway lay directly before him. Inside, a

128

dim light bulb illuminated the interior of the tiniest cell he'd ever seen. The prospect of being confined to this stark concrete box terrified him, but he was too shocked and too proud to let his captors see it.

Jerry heard a voice behind him: "How do you like your new home?" He turned and saw Rat grinning at him.

"No one can stand this," Jerry said.

Rat didn't reply. Guards pushed Jerry toward the cell's interior. With no choice, he shuffled his weighted feet across the threshold, leaving the world outside, perhaps forever. Rat closed the door, sealing Jerry in what he feared would become his tomb.

Jerry heard the guards leave and the noise subside. Alone, he looked around the new home the Camp Authority had given him. He wondered, *How much more can I take? What is honor worth?* He felt a choking sensation in his throat; the walls seemed to press against him. He heard the skittering of roaches along the floor. He looked around in disbelief, then horror. He stood on a patch of concrete flooring that measured forty-eight inches square—four feet long by four feet wide. He stretched out his left arm, then his right. Both hands touched the sides of his cell. An elevated concrete sleeping platform rose at one end of the four-by-four concrete floor and stretched six feet to the back of the cell. On the platform, guards had laid a pathetically thin sleeping pallet, made of dirty bamboo strips. A nail protruded precisely where his right shoulder should lay. A faint light bulb, ten watts or less he surmised, plunged the four-by-ten-foot space into a permanent twilight.

He turned toward the door and saw a peephole in the heavy wood, but no window. Above the door he saw a metal plate perforated with a number of small holes for ventilation. Two electrical wires snaked through one of the holes, feeding the bulb and a small speaker. He felt sure the speaker would soon pump Hanoi Hannah's diatribe straight into his cell. A slight breeze brushed his toes, and he noticed a six-inch space beneath the door. Tomorrow, he thought, he could curl himself on the floor and see outside.

Next, he inventoried his belongings, which a guard had tossed onto the floor behind him. He had a toothbrush but no toothpaste, a water jug, and a porcelain drinking cup. He had a hard piece of soap and washrag. Two sets of underwear and two shirts were on the platform along with a turtleneck sweatshirt and pair of rubber sandals; he had no socks for his feet. A torn mosquito net would offer some protection against the nighttime insects drawn to the cell's light; maddeningly, more insects than air seemed to pass through the cell's few openings. Finally, he had the one item that had accompanied him since the day he arrived in Hanoi more than two years ago: a latrine bucket, with all its filth, odor, and humiliation. Once again, Jerry found himself without any control over his circumstance. And once again, he would call upon all his resources to handle it as best he could.

He could survive any ordeal with the support of his men. Even sporadic messages or taps were enough to screw up his determination, to remind him that others counted on his example. Had the Camp Authority isolated this group of POWs from the Hanoi Hilton *and* from each other, he didn't know how long he'd survive. Then, this cell might truly become his grave. Could he make contact?

He said a prayer, put his cup to the wall, his ear to the cup, and tapped, "Denton." In response, he heard "McKnight." George McKnight, who'd made a legendary fifteen-mile escape, was next to him. He soon learned McKnight's accomplice, George Coker, occupied the next cell. Jerry had heard rumors of how the two POWs had picked the locks to their cuffs and escaped from a small prison near the Red River two weeks earlier. They'd swum fifteen miles toward the Gulf of Tonkin before being apprehended. Their stunt apparently earned them a place in this new prison, which Jerry began to suspect the

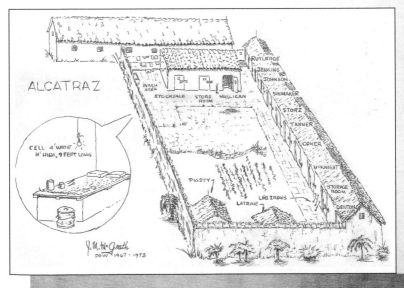

Diagram of Alcatraz, which imprisoned and isolated the eleven leading American POWs, 1967–1969. Sketch by former POW Mike McGrath.

Camp Authority had reserved for its most problematic characters.

Jerry soon had the new facility's lineup. In the first cell, near the entrance, lived navy commander Howie Rutledge. Progressively closer to Jerry were navy commander Harry Jenkins, air force major Sam Johnson, navy lieutenant commander Bob Shumaker, air force captain Ron Storz, navy lieutenant commander Nels Tanner, young navy lieutenant junior grade George Coker, and air force captain George McKnight, all in solitary from what Jerry could tell. Jerry Denton was senior officer and at the end of what the Camp Authority must have considered an actual murderers' row. Jerry realized the Camp Authority had sequestered nearly the entire gang of troublemakers from Stardust, except for Jim Stockdale and Jim Mulligan. What had Cat done with them?

The next morning, Jerry awoke at what he guessed was 6:30 a.m. For twenty-seven months, he'd never been entirely certain of the time, except on the rare occasions when he glimpsed the face of an officer's wristwatch. He heard jingling keys and soft commands in the courtyard. A door opened and closed. He crawled from his pallet and curled up on his four-by-four standing area. Leg irons made this even more difficult. He peered under the door into the dawn. He saw a scraggly courtyard surrounded by a yellowish stucco wall, what looked like a concrete latrine almost directly before him, and a pigsty in the opposite corner. One look at the freely wallowing pigs reminded him even livestock in Hanoi fared better than he did. At least the hogs served a purpose, he thought. After two years of resisting to no apparent end, and being no closer to going home, Jerry confronted the creeping specter of purposelessness. Did all their resistance and all their suffering have a point?

In the far corner of the small compound, he spied a trough and cistern next to a small tile-roofed building with three cell doors. Suddenly, a guard escorted Jim Stockdale out of the door on the far left. The two senior officers had communicated through notes, taps, and whispers but hadn't laid eyes on each other in Hanoi. Jerry knew Stockdale would serve as senior officer; Jerry would serve as executive officer, second in command. Jerry's former Naval Academy classmate looked haggard and old; Jerry wondered if prison life had aged his own countenance so harshly. The commander's left leg appeared stiff and he swung it awkwardly as he hobbled across the yard; Jerry attributed the limp to an ejection injury coupled with local medical care. Stockdale climbed up the latrine's two steps, bringing his bum leg with him. He emptied his bucket into the hole as his guard watched with disinterest. Jerry had known Stockdale since age eighteen; to many POWs he was simply a name, however. To make sure everyone in the compound knew his identity, Stockdale washed out his bucket methodically, using the brush to scrape out "Stockdale" in code: "scrape, scrape, scrape, scrape—pause—scrape, scrape, scrape" for S, and so forth. Ten minutes later, the guard returned Stockdale to his cell. Then the guard unlocked the small building's third door and pulled out Jim Mulligan. God, it was good to see Jim and his big sideburns.

After Jim Mulligan used the latrine, guards brought out a POW Jerry had never seen. The guard led the prisoner to the latrine where he used a brush to scrape out "Howie Rutledge." Jerry recognized the name as the fellow navy commander in cell 1 of Jerry's cellblock. Next came a gangly six-foot-five POW who seemed unable to hold a straight face: Harry Jenkins. Jerry guessed the rail-thin specter that came next was cell 3's Sam Johnson, the Texan who Jerry had learned flew lead solo for the US Air Force Thunderbirds. The guard next brought into Jerry's view a freckled, boyish face. The young man moved along efficiently and used the brush to communicate a stream of rapid abbreviations Jerry strained to translate. Jerry caught "Shumaker." Jerry had learned the reputedly brilliant naval aviator had nearly spent the war with NASA's Apollo astronaut program. An enlarged lymph node had cost him his place in the program, however, so he was spending the war in Hanoi and now occupied this new prison's cell 4.

Next, Jerry got his first glimpse of Ron Storz, whom he remembered from his first months in the Hanoi Hilton. Jerry noted Ron's striking blue eyes; he also noticed their evident melancholy. Later, when Ron bathed, Jerry saw the remnants of a once-impressive physique. Sadly, even the strongest men succumbed to a diet of cold soup.

Guards brought into view a POW who scraped out "Nels Tanner." Jerry recognized him as author of the "Superman Confession." Earlier in the year, Nels had signed a statement naming Superman's alias, Clark Kent, as his squadron commander. He'd named television character Ben Casey as a wingman. Cat publicized the confession, unwittingly embarrassing the Camp Authority on an international level. Nels paid a stiff price when Cat learned about his subterfuge. He'd become a celebrated legend among the POWs.

The guard escorted Tanner out of Jerry's field of view and returned with a trim, five-foot-six, baby-faced POW who looked like actor James Cagney. He scraped "George Coker." Coker's fellow escapee, George McKnight, walked into view next. The six-foot boxer and air force captain still walked with a swagger. The look on his face clearly said, *Don't mess with me.* Jerry took great joy in knowing what his compatriots looked like— especially after knowing them as only names for so long. He knew these men had to carry one another through the ordeal they'd face in exile at Alcatraz.

The guard came for Jerry last. He released Jerry's leg irons and the commander stepped into daylight, seeing his surroundings from eye level for the first time. He confirmed his was the last cell in a building with ten cell doors facing the courtyard. He ran through the nine men from his cellblock: Rutledge, Jenkins, Johnson, Shumaker, Storz, Tanner, Coker, McKnight, Denton; he wondered if a tenth man stood silently behind one of his building's ten doors. He'd also seen Stockdale and Mulligan exit two doors in a three-door building across the courtyard; the middle door had remained closed. Perhaps the North Vietnamese were using the empty cell in each building to foil communication. Considering how faint McKnight's taps seemed, Jerry deduced the empty cell in his building was next to him. The Camp Authority must have aimed to isolate him entirely.

Outside at the latrine, Jerry identified himself as the others had. When he finished cleaning his bucket, it stank only slightly less than it had before. Jerry started to return to his cell, but the guard indicated he should wash down the latrine. Jerry complied, then the guard locked him away. His cleaning duties at least allowed him several additional minutes outside his shoebox of a cell.

Around what he estimated as 10:30 a.m., Jerry heard footsteps, jingling keys, and the clanking of bowls. He'd heard the sound so many times that his mouth reflexively watered. Denton silently cursed his captors; they'd turned him into a Pavlovian dog. He felt almost more animal than man.

Footsteps neared and a bowl slid under his door. In it sloshed watery soup with stringy greens and bits of rice and pork fat. No different from the food he'd received everywhere else. And just like he'd done at nearly every meal in North Vietnam, he pounced on the food and slurped it straight from the bowl. As he licked remnants from his stubble, he was just as hungry as he'd been before the food arrived.

After guards collected the bowls from beneath each door, Jerry heard sweeping. He noticed a deliberate cadence and recognized the tap code. He peered under his heavy door, and eventually Bob Shumaker, surrounded by a small cloud of dust, came into sight. Shumaker had apparently been tasked with sweeping the packed-dirt yard. The sandy-haired whiz kid didn't waste a stroke as he worked his way around the compound, broadcasting as he went. Each sweep of the broom sent a message in tap code. For Jerry and the POWs, Bob Shumaker was Walter Cronkite—although Shu's knowledge extended only to happenings at 4 Lý Nam Đế; anything else was opinionated speculation.

That afternoon, McKnight relayed taps from George Coker. "This place is like Alcatraz," Coker sent. "What a lockdown." The cellblock's residents immediately liked the name. Coker requested Jerry's approval and the POWs christened their new prison Alcatraz.

Jerry, like his fellow inmates, took some pride in being banished here. Members of the Alcatraz Gang, as they called their band, had distinguished themselves as fanatical resisters, troublemakers, and persistently subversive leaders. The Camp Authority apparently considered them beyond hope of reform. They surely considered them their absolute worst POWs. America would consider them its best.

The day passed without event. In fact, *nothing* happened. Jerry realized how difficult passing time might become in this isolated little dungeon. The late afternoon feeding, which he estimated came around 4:30 p.m., offered the same fare as breakfast. After guards collected the licked-clean bowls, Jerry heard the clank of iron. He heard barks of anger from other POWs; guards were issuing leg irons. Soon, his own door opened and a guard clamped iron cuffs around his legs and locked them to a metal bar. The Camp Authority had already locked him behind a heavy padlocked door; the irons were a needless slap. Jerry lay down on his mat with his legs in irons and the dim light bulb still burning. Eventually, despite his discomfort, he dozed off wondering how long this exile would last.

With no other choice, the Alcatraz Gang began settling into the daily routine foisted upon them. It began with sounds of daybreak. Yawns, coughs, and hacks came from the captives who were always slightly ill. These sounds would wake Jerry, who hoped, just for a moment before opening his eyes, he might be back aboard *Independence*. Could this be a dream? The cheery voice of Hanoi Hannah would remind him that it wasn't. Her propaganda helped the POWs start each day on the wrong foot.

Activity in the streets would gradually increase; sounds of happiness and commerce floated over the wall, reminding Jerry life went on outside Alcatraz. The first POW to visit the latrine would usually deliver a weather report. Even though the POWs would spend their entire day locked inside windowless boxes, much discussion was given to the conditions outside. Other messages delivered in morning soliloquies included birthday wishes and reminders of anniversaries. In their bizarre world, anniversaries were not of marriages but of shootdowns. "HAG," Jerry scraped out on November 6: *Happy anniversary, George McKnight.* By necessity, the POWs became exceptionally proficient at shorthand code. Each man in Alcatraz adopted a one-letter name. Jim Stockdale claimed S and Jim Mulligan took M. Howie Rutledge had H, Harry Jenkins was J, and Sam Johnson took L, since his seniors had both S and J. Bob Shumaker, Ron Storz, and Nels Tanner had B, R, and T, respectively. Escapees George Coker and George McKnight picked C and G. Jerry claimed D for Denton.

Seven days later, Jerry heard someone send "Swish, swish—swish, swish, swish—pause—swish—swish, swish—pause—swish, swish—swish, swish, swish." He translated "HBH": *Happy birthday, Howie Rutledge.* For the POWs, birthdays were less painful than anniversaries. Anniversaries reminded them how long they'd been in Hanoi.

Jerry usually ended Alcatraz's morning latrine rituals with a benediction as he washed down the area. He often included new orders and policies. His congregants quickly tired of directives; orders seemed to have little relevance to men locked in tiny cells with no immediate prospects for release. When that feedback came tapping hotly down the walls to Jerry, he shifted direction. The next day, he brushed out, "In Thy gentle hands, we are smiling our thanks." His men approved.

Sometimes, Jerry's orations ran long. One day, he focused so hard on a lengthy tap code soliloquy that he failed to hear Rat approaching. Suddenly, he sensed the commandant's presence behind him. He turned around and saw Rat grinning. "Denton," he said, "that is a very long message."

At the end of his first week, when Jerry finished cleaning the latrine, a guard led him to the cistern and trough near Stockdale's cell. The guard indicated he should strip and wash. He pulled off his pajamas and boxers and stood naked in the middle of the camp. He dumped cold water on himself. In the late autumn air, the chilly water felt as pleasant as Pigeye's fists. Yet it at least helped rinse away a layer of filth. He tried to extract some lather from his sliver of soap, but the water temperature made that even more difficult. He did his best to spread the lather over his body with a thin washrag. Then he dumped water on himself again. Shivering against the cold, he washed his pajamas in the trough and hung them to dry. He slipped on spare shorts that the guard had brought and trudged back to his cell. He berated himself for feeling gratitude to his captors for letting him bathe.

———

Jerry had endured two years of solitary already, but the isolation of Alcatraz proved even more demoralizing. No new POWs arrived with news from outside. Nobody transferred in or out. Almost no interrogations occurred, so he had no opportunity to fight. Nothing at all happened. Minutes seemed to last hours. Seconds seemed to last minutes. Even at the Hilton and the Zoo, Jerry had never felt time pass so slowly or depression settle so heavily upon him. He struggled to endure this psychological torture.

He began to retreat inward for long periods of time. Daily, he recited his list of POWs in Hanoi. He learned that most other prisoners did the same. Jim Mulligan's alphabetized list of POWs had stopped growing as of their move to Alcatraz in October 1967, but he had more than three hundred to recite and share. Jerry also undertook the detailed mental construction of an elaborate home. He created lists of materials and contractors, architectural plans, and imagined the house being built brick by brick and joint by joint. He also worked complicated mathematic equations entirely in his head. One day when he tried to communicate with another POW, he got a message back: "Call me later, I'm working on something." POWs did their best to pass excruciatingly long minutes, hours, and days. They'd spend prodigious blocks of time immersed in mental exercises and journeys into memory.

In the mornings and at night, Jerry would think about his wife, Jane, and his family. He'd let himself dwell briefly on those pleasant memories. Occasionally, he'd even relive his meeting Jane on a summer hayride shortly after he graduated from McGill. A classmate brought Jane as his date; Jerry brought another girl. Sixteen-year-old Jane Maury quickly caught his eye, however, and he forgot about his own date. Something sparked between the two. Jerry decided he'd met his wife. Jane graduated as valedictorian of the Convent of Visitation School in Mobile and enrolled at Mary Washington College in northern Virginia, not far from Annapolis. The day after Jerry graduated from the Naval Academy—June 6, 1946—he married Jane in the Naval Academy Chapel. The two walked through the arch of sabers formed by Jerry's classmates and began an extraordinary life together. Jerry could not dwell on that life now, however. He prayed for his family only at dawn and dusk; otherwise he locked away their memory and focused on getting his men through their present ordeal.

Jerry eventually began indexing former colleagues and classmates, which he found less painful than thinking of his family. He started with his squadron, VA-75, aboard *Independence*. Then he reconstructed his US Naval Academy class, name by name, face by face. High school came next. Within several months, Jerry was reassembling yearbooks and desk arrangements from elementary school. Long-forgotten names and faces miraculously returned. Other POWs experienced similar phenomena; Stockdale flashed across the yard, "We are regressing. We're going back to our childhoods." Indeed, Jerry wallowed in childhood memories; he spent hours recalling a riding airplane he received for his third birthday. He imagined himself riding the toy through the hotel his parents managed. He considered how fascination with flight had ultimately led him to fight his war on the ground, locked in a cell in North Vietnam.

Jerry found sleep difficult. Other than running in place, he had virtually no physical activity to tire his body. Yet even if he'd had an entire gymnasium at his disposal, his meager rations wouldn't have fueled any exercise of worth. The constantly burning light bulb added another challenge. Leg irons added one more. He could either sleep flat on his back or flat on his stomach. His thin bamboo mat scarcely softened the concrete underneath it. And there was the one protruding nail, right at his shoulder.

To pass late night hours, Jerry turned to his only companions:

gecko lizards, spiders, ants, and mosquitoes. He observed that a large male seemed to run the gecko colony; he nicknamed him "Bullmoose." He concocted a veritable soap opera around Bullmoose as he darted across the ceiling, catching mosquitoes, courting females, and producing the next generation of geckos. Not all of Bullmoose's offspring thrived. Jerry would swat mosquitoes and feed the insects to the weakest lizards. Once he downed a mosquito, Jerry had to collect it before the cell's other inhabitants descended upon it. If he didn't, ants would arrive first. A spider usually came next, taking the ants' prize. An adult gecko typically showed up last, eating spider *and* mosquito. For Jerry, the cell's food chain became his television. Too bad, Jerry thought, that the geckos showed little interest in the flies blanketing his walls.

In his hours alone, Jerry devised a variant of the POW tap code. The men were so sick that he figured the guards wouldn't think anything of coughs and sneezes. He issued new signals for the grid coordinates used for tap code. One or two coughs signified 1 or 2. Clearing a throat meant 3. A loud hock was 4 and a loud sneeze or spit indicated 5. The new system gained favor. Jerry figured the guards must have thought the POWs were near death given the volume of bodily noise coming from Alcatraz.

Chapter 10

1968

ONE DAY IN DECEMBER, Rat unexpectedly opened Jerry's door. He poked his head inside and asked, "Denton, what would you like for Christmas?" The question stunned Jerry. He recovered and asked for a letter from home. Rat left without committing. Jerry heard him proceed to other cells. POWs tapped encounters up and down the cellblock. Howie Rutledge's quick response got a laugh from Jerry: "A cup of coffee and a bus ticket to Saigon." Saigon was the capital of America's ally South Vietnam.

On Christmas Day, Rat brought most of the requested gifts to the POWs; the men tapped their surprise and details about their loot. Jerry received a priceless letter from Jane; his first in two and a half years. He devoured Jane's letter and read it time and again. The gentle handwritten words brought tears of joy and pain. Jerry missed his family dearly. They'd had no contact since July 1965. He knew Jane would remain faithful, he knew his children would remember him. Still, every man had lingering doubts about how his family would endure such a separation and how they'd receive him when he returned, if he returned. After reading the letter, however, Jerry locked away their memory so he could survive the day. Thinking of his family too often would have crushed him.

On that Christmas of 1967, all the men received a meal of turkey, egg rolls, spiced salad, and caramel candy. Jerry ate it all, his shrunken stomach somehow expanding to handle the rare serving of real food. As Jerry lay in his cell, belly bloated with Christmas dinner, Rat appeared again. He handed Jerry a paper chessboard and told him he could play only by himself; he was not to communicate. Other POWs received the boards and soon the walls were alive with taps from POWs playing one another. Occasionally, Jerry would hear shouts like "You dirty bastard!" He knew one POW had outfoxed another. When POWs grew weary of chess, Five Questions became the game of choice. POWs would tap to a partner and pose a question such as "Name five fish that can live in both salt and fresh water." Vicious debates often ensued and other POWs joined in. The men placed heavy wagers on their answers and opinions. Bets were always payable in cash or food upon homecoming, whenever that might be.

In her January 30, 1968, broadcast, Hanoi Hannah asked American soldiers, "Why do you want to fight against the just cause of Vietnam? You can see you are losing. Lay down your arms! Refuse to fight! Demand to be taken home, now! Today! Do you want to die in a foreign land, eight thousand miles from your home?"

It was Tết, the Vietnamese New Year. And from Hannah, the POWs in Alcatraz learned North Vietnam and the Việt Cộng had launched an eighty-thousand-man offensive across South Vietnam. Their troops and insurgents staged simultaneous attacks on five of six major cities, thirty-six of forty-four provincial capitals, and numerous other targets, including unprepared or unaware US bases. Việt Cộng guerrillas even attacked the US Embassy and held a portion of its grounds for six hours. The violence and scale of the attacks shocked the American public, who had been led by the Johnson administration to believe that America was winning the war. The news delighted Hanoi Hannah. She did not report the final assessment of the attack, however: US and South Vietnamese forces had rallied and generally claimed victory. But the real victory, in accordance with North Vietnam's strategy, was turning American public opinion against the war in Vietnam. The Tết Offensive accomplished that goal.

A February 1 image by photojournalist Eddie Adams dealt a blow almost as powerful as Tết to support for what was becoming known as President Johnson's war. Adams snapped a vivid and chilling photo of South Vietnam's national police chief summarily executing a suspected Việt Cộng insurgent. Americans wondered what madness gripped Vietnam. After Tết 1968, the people of the United States began losing confidence in the war.

Jerry didn't trust the reports from Radio Hanoi, but he knew something was up. And it didn't sound good. A message came down from Sam Johnson in cell 3. Rabbit had visited and walked him through an Alcatraz quiz room covered with photographs of Communist victories during the Tết Offensive and of increasing domestic turmoil in the United States. Images were harder to discount than Hannah's diatribe.

"Your country has deserted you," Sam reported Rabbit saying. "You will never go home. You have been left here to die."

Jim Stockdale responded from across the courtyard, "The US will never give up on us."

"Never happen," agreed Jerry. "They won't leave us here." Jerry hoped this promise helped his men. At heart, he had begun struggling to believe it himself. For the next three months, Hanoi Hannah brought selective reports of the Tết Offensive and its aftermath; none lifted the POWs' spirits. How, with more than five hundred thousand troops in South Vietnam, was the United States losing the war?

Hannah delivered another blow when she announced that Hanoi had released three American POWs on February 16, 1968. Hannah broadcast their conciliatory statements; they thanked North Vietnam for its kindness and good treatment. Jerry nearly exploded with fury. He and Stockdale had been isolated only four months and the POW organization was clearly disintegrating. How could leaders have allowed men to accept an unconscionable early release? What happened to their bedrock edict, "We all go home together"?

At February's end, Hannah brought still more demoralizing tidings. She reported a devastating statement from revered news anchor Walter Cronkite, who'd recently returned from a trip to Vietnam. "To say that we are mired in stalemate seems the only realistic, yet unsatisfactory, conclusion," Cronkite had announced on national television. "It is increasingly clear to this reporter that the only rational way out then will be to negotiate, not as victors, but as honorable people who lived up to their pledge to defend democracy, and did the best they could." It seemed Americans were giving up on victory in Vietnam. What would that mean for the POWs?

To men struggling to find purpose and clinging to hope of an eventual homecoming, the Tết Offensive, early releases, and Cronkite's eulogy stung. Jerry and others couldn't help but question their perceptions and their mission. The news undermined their bedrock belief that America would win. They wondered what was truly happening in the big world outside their tiny cells. Three and a half years removed from the real war, they wondered if their mission and their sacrifice were still relevant. Despite creeping doubts, they *had* to believe both still mattered.

Uncertainty outside encouraged POWs to seek certainty within themselves. Jerry ensured that the men worshipped on Sundays, and he personally gave himself to prayer, spending hours on his knees. He'd pray the rosary again and again; he'd meditate upon its meaning. The Alcatraz Gang declared a Sunday in March as Easter 1968, and Jerry Denton composed a three-stanza poem. He had no paper, so he composed the verses in his mind.

He delivered the stanzas one at a time, on Holy Thursday, Good Friday, and Holy Saturday.

1968

THE GREAT SIGN

HIS MANGER BIRTH DREW KINGS IN AWE,
HIS SMILE THE FORMER BLIND MEN SAW,
IN HIM DIVINE AND MORTAL MERGED,
YET HE'S THE ONE THE SOLDIERS SCOURGED.

HE PRAISED THE HUMBLE AND THE MEEK,
THE GRATEFUL DEAF-MUTE HEARD HIM SPEAK,
HIS FACE WAS LOVE PERSONIFIED,
YET HE'S THE ONE THEY CRUCIFIED.

NOW OUR TEARS WITH DOUBTS COMBINE,
HOW COULD HE DIE YET BE DIVINE?
WE MUST DISPEL THIS FAITHLESS GLOOM,
LET'S PRAY AT DAWN BESIDE HIS TOMB.

The poem's title, "The Great Sign," applied to the POWs too. Jerry frantically searched for some indication their situation would change. He thought he received it on April 1. While passing time in his cell that afternoon, he suddenly heard keys jingle. The door opened and Rat stood in his doorway, beaming. "Denton, we have defeated you! There will be no more bombing! Johnson has quit!"

Rat grinned and left Jerry alone. He immediately relayed the experience via taps. He suggested Rat had spun a major North Vietnamese concession. Jerry assumed Hồ Chí Minh gave in and Johnson stopped bombing North Vietnam in response. He felt lighthearted for once; his miserable sentence would soon end. Homecoming was nigh.

Later that day, Hanoi Hannah's broadcast helped explain Rat's statement. Jerry and his men heard their commander in chief's voice come through the speakers in their cells: "Tonight, I renew the offer I made last August—to stop the bombardment of North Vietnam. We ask that talks begin promptly, that they be serious talks on the substance of peace." Every POW in Alcatraz wondered, would a bombing halt and peace talks lead to homecoming? The president continued and Jerry understood what Rat meant when he said Johnson had quit. The president's Texas accent intoned, "I shall not seek, and I will not accept, the nomination of my party for another term as your president." Not seeking a second term was an effective resignation. The POWs were shocked. Johnson had given up.

Ever optimistic, Jerry still took the bombing halt as the great sign for which he'd prayed. A halt meant peace. Peace would mean release. Maybe 1968 would see them home.

⎯⎯⎯⎯

As 1968 continued, days in Alcatraz remained unchanged. Hannah made no more mention of peace. The bombing halt seemed less like a prelude to peace and more like a chance for North Vietnam to recover and extend the war. Jerry's hope for peace and return began to dissipate. Of more immediate concern, his cell began to grow hotter by the day. Hanoi's summer had arrived in May. On sunny days, he could feel heat pulsing through the unprotected roof. He sweated out every ounce of water he drank. He'd sit quietly, trying not to move, watching drops of sweat drip and trace down his arms and chest. The air above his bunk would grow too thick and hot to breathe. It forced him to the floor, where he spent his afternoons sucking air from beneath his door.

Jerry heard taps coming through the wall from George McKnight, who was relaying a message from George Coker, who was relaying a message from Nels Tanner. Tanner served as the relay between Jerry's nine-man cellblock and the two-man block shared by Jim Stockdale and Jim Mulligan. Tanner's cell had a perfect angle to see Stockdale or Mulligan flash their hands in code beneath their doors. Jerry knew that meant Tanner spent hours curled uncomfortably on his floor being the communication link between the two Alcatraz cellblocks. On this occasion Tanner had relayed a message from Jim Mulligan to Jerry, sending it down the cellblock via George Coker and George McKnight.

Mulligan reported Cat had visited camp and called him to quiz. Rat and Cat had asked about Mulligan's condition and his recent refusal to eat. Mulligan had stripped off his shirt and ranted, "My bones are showing, I'm starving, and I can't eat. I can't breathe and you ask me why I won't eat."

Jerry realized his men could not survive much longer. He needed to act, and he considered how to approach Rat; a straightforward demand would never work. At his next encounter, Jerry told the commandant, "I want to congratulate you on carrying through on the excruciating treatment and putting us to a slow death by heat."

"No, Denton," Rat responded, with surprise. "I did not know conditions were that bad. Our orders are to keep you isolated and in irons. We have no orders to kill you. We will study."

The next day, Tanner relayed that Rat and Cat had visited Mulligan's cell to assess the temperature. Mulligan reported that one guard nearly burned himself when he touched the sunbaked door. Cat and Rat had promised to address the extreme heat. Soon thereafter, Jerry heard new voices in the courtyard. He dropped to the floor and watched a work detail begin removing the metal plates above the doors to Stockdale's and Mulligan's cells. They disappeared from his view as they began, presumably, doing the same for his own nine-man cellblock. Finally, the crew arrived outside Jerry's cell. They entered and removed the bolts from the plate's top, then bent it inward, parallel to the ceiling. Light and a breeze flowed into Jerry's oppressive hovel. The next day, the workers returned. Jerry watched and listened as they added a thatched second roof to shield his cellblock from the sun. They also planted vines outside his door. On his daily visits to the latrine, he watched the vines climb upward all along the cellblock, providing precious leafy shade as they grew. He and his men were still trapped inside tiny cells, but at least they could now survive the summer.

Summer of 1968 brought a new administrator to Alcatraz; the POWs named him "Slick." The warden's first contribution was erecting a screen around the bath area to afford POWs a hint of privacy while they bathed. He also instituted an extra ten minutes of outdoor exercise each day and baths became daily instead of weekly. Otherwise, nothing at Alcatraz changed. The days passed slowly, the hours and minutes seemed to pass even slower. Hope of homecoming was fading with the changing seasons. At least torture had abated, so days passed in a less physically painful manner.

———

One morning in mid-December, Jerry Denton heard taps coming from George McKnight. He leaned his cup against the wall to amplify the sound, listened, then responded. Suddenly, he heard McKnight's door being pulled open. A guard yelled, "You communicate!" Seconds later, Jerry's door flew open. The same guard shouted, "You communicate!" A chill ran through Jerry's body. For fourteen months, communication had gone largely ignored by Alcatraz administrators and guards. Now, a sudden change. His door slammed shut.

Jerry heard guards drag McKnight from his cell; he watched from underneath his door until they moved out of his field of view. He suspected orders had come for confessions and biographies. That would mean torture. Jerry began to pray.

POWs could hear any sound made inside the Alcatraz courtyard. Five days later, Jerry heard an American walking and looked out to see McKnight being led to the latrine. He looked terrible. As he scraped out his bucket, he broadcast he'd been tortured for a letter of apology to the Vietnamese people. Back in his cell, he tapped to Jerry: "Purge, I say no comm."

Knowing the POWs needed communication like they needed water, Jerry responded, "Keep the volume up and if you get caught, you tell them that I *ordered* you to do it."

Just as Jerry finished his message, his door opened and the same guards who'd returned McKnight hauled out Jerry. They took him outside the courtyard and into a quiz room. There he found Mickey Mouse, whom he remembered well from his session with Pigeye at the Hilton. Jerry feared the Mouse's arrival portended a revival of harsh treatment.

"You have been caught communicating," declared the new warden. "You must apologize. You must write letter to President Hồ Chí Minh and apologize for your crimes."

Yes, old times had returned. The Camp Authority once again used punishment as an excuse to extract a statement. Jerry refused the request.

"Okay," Mickey Mouse replied. "I leave you to think deeply."

A guard locked irons around Jerry's ankles and pushed him against a wall. He received instructions to keep his hands raised over his head. A guard stood nearby to ensure he complied. After three days, Mickey Mouse returned to find Jerry with his hands still raised. He asked if Jerry would write an apology. Jerry still refused.

"We are going to get serious, then, Denton," said the officer. Jerry knew he meant it.

Mickey Mouse left and Jerry used a pencil to scratch out a note stating they'd have to torture him to death before he wrote an apology to Hồ Chí Minh or anyone else. Signing the note, he knew pain would come. He also knew he'd once again be fighting for his country and his honor. Purpose had returned.

As soon as Mickey Mouse came back and read Jerry's note, he ordered guards to apply rear cuffs and leg irons. One guard dragged the bound and helpless prisoner across the hard floor. As Jerry's ankles and wrists scraped along, the iron bands dug into his flesh. Eventually, the guard left him on the floor, with no food, water, or bucket. Hours passed. The next time the door opened, Mickey Mouse walked in and appraised his captive. He offered Jerry another chance to write. Jerry said, "No."

Three guards entered. One held a rope and a pole. The threesome bound Jerry's forearms and spread his elbows wide. They pushed his knees through the resulting space, so his chin nearly rested on his kneecaps. His bent back immediately ached. He learned the pole's purpose when the guards threaded it through the diamonds of space created between his bent knees and elbows. The guards propped him on his spine and placed his feet on a block, about one foot off the floor. Then they left. The rig pressed Jerry's thighs so tightly against his lungs that he could barely breathe. His neck and spine radiated pain. Yet Jerry hacked it for four hours.

When Mickey Mouse returned, he ordered Jerry untied and food brought. Jerry still wouldn't write. "Denton, we will break you now," Mickey Mouse said.

A new guard entered and tied Jerry into the rig tighter than ever. His hands turned black. He passed out. A guard loosened the rig and blood streamed back into starved arteries and tissues, causing a terrific pain. The guards kept up the cycle. Mickey Mouse visited during this new session and watched several guards beat Jerry.

As he approached twelve hours of constant pain, Jerry thought, *I would run my own mother down with a truck if the price was freedom from pain.* He felt his heart struggle to pump blood through his constricted limbs. He had a strange yet honest thought: He hoped his heart would just wear out so he could die and Mickey Mouse could never make him write that damned apology. Jerry Denton began praying to die. The Lord did not grant the request. When he could stand the pain no longer, he had no choice but to give up. He weakly croaked for a guard. Mickey Mouse looked triumphant when he arrived. Jerry agreed to write. The guards released his bonds and left him on the cold concrete floor.

The next day, December 23, 1968, he wrote three brief paragraphs apologizing, in the vaguest of ways, to Hồ Chí Minh. He was sure Hanoi Hannah and the Hanoi press would soon broadcast his words for all to hear. He felt humiliated.

Jerry had just begun to recover in his cell when, the next evening, guards barged in, stood him up, and blindfolded him. With help, he stumbled out of the Alcatraz courtyard and along the street outside. His legs loosened up, and he gradually began walking under his own power. Guards removed the blindfold and he recognized the building where he'd blinked out TORTURE in Morse code during his interview two and a half years ago. He was forty-one years old then. Now he felt at least seventy.

Jerry entered the big house and walked into a brightly lit room with a decadent table at its center. Trays of food and drink, even champagne, covered the table. Jerry looked for cameras; he suspected the Camp Authority staged the event for propaganda photographs. The commandant of the North Vietnamese prison system walked up and greeted him cheerily. "Ah, Denton, good to see you again," said Cat. "How are you?"

Jerry gruffly responded he'd just been tortured.

Cat paid no mind. "How are conditions?"

"Terrible," Jerry said. "Can't eat because of the torture."

"Is there anything I can do for you?"

"Only if you do it for everyone," he replied, referencing the Code of Conduct's prohibition of special favors. Jerry saw Cat begin to simmer, and the two leaders both grew angrier by the word. Cat attempted to salvage the dialogue and offered Jerry a banana. Jerry declined.

Voice rising, Cat said, "All right, Denton, eat that banana!" He pointed at the table.

"No." Jerry was still incensed about the letter he'd had to sign and wasn't feeling cooperative.

"It will be good for you."

"If everyone gets a banana, I will take it."

"Shut mouth!" Cat yelled. "You eat banana! That is an order!"

Jerry shook his head emphatically. Both men were livid. Cat sent him back to Alcatraz.

Chapter 11

CHANGE

JERRY HAD NEVER BEEN AFRAID to stand up for principle in a fight. The incident with Cat made him recall two instances in Virginia Beach where he'd stood firm. He dove into those memories to help pass time as 1968 became 1969.

He coached his sons' sports teams whenever he could, although long deployments made him miss many games. One fall, he was coaching his son Billy's football team when a young black player tried out. A local Virginia Beach politico would not allow a black player to participate. That rubbed Jerry the wrong way. He drove to the kingpin's office, barged in, and slammed his fist on the man's desk. "By God, that young man *will* be on my team," he yelled, "and I don't want to hear anything else about it!" The young man became team captain.

Another time, his son Billy came home crying. A friend's father had threatened to spank him. Furious, Jerry called the other father, whom he'd never met. He loosed a tirade and made it exceedingly clear that nobody would spank Billy except him.

He hung up the phone and composed himself. He looked at Billy, swallowed hard, and asked, "So, how big is that guy?" Jerry always stood up for his principles and his family, no matter the adversary or cost. In Hanoi, the Code of Conduct was his principle and the POWs were his family.

On January 8, 1969, guards escorted Jerry to Mickey Mouse's office. Mickey Mouse calmly asked Jerry what had happened on Christmas Eve. Jerry responded that he had just followed the Code of Conduct, which forbids accepting favors.

"You were a fool on Christmas Eve, Denton," Mickey Mouse said. "Now you must pay. You must read on the camp radio."

Mickey Mouse had Jerry put straight into the rope-and-pole rig. He purposefully left the room's windows open so the Alcatraz inmates could hear Jerry's screams and groans. The men of Alcatraz listened to their fellow POW suffer for two days. When Jerry surrendered, he spasmed on the floor so badly that Mickey Mouse called a doctor.

As soon as Jerry had stabilized, Mickey Mouse pushed a script into his hands. Jerry tried to recite it, but his mind and body were so wasted from two days of torture that nobody could understand his garbled words. Mickey Mouse tried again the next day. Jerry's words were still hoarse and slurred, but Mickey Mouse accepted them. Jerry was thankful he seemed not to notice several deliberate and egregious mispronunciations. The Alcatraz POWs certainly did, however. When Jerry's forced words came over the camp speakers, along with phrases like "Horseshit Minh" instead of Hồ Chí Minh, Jerry heard his men laugh.

Mickey Mouse shut off the recording. Guards took Jerry back to his cell, where he recounted the story on the wall. He elaborated, "They want us to write letters asking Hồ Chí Minh for amnesty. If they're working on some kind of release, they can't just turn us loose without losing face. They have to have some kind of justification, some kind of admission of guilt. Then Uncle Hồ can forgive us. Don't make it easy for them. Hold out as long as you can." Jerry's resilience and optimism proved boundless. Maybe, he thought, this round of torture meant release was closer.

The next day, Jerry heard that Jim Mulligan had been hauled out. Mulligan returned within the day and reported via Nels Tanner. Mulligan had refused to read a script and told Mickey Mouse, "You tortured [Denton] badly, and if you want me to read, you'll have to torture me the same way." Mickey Mouse had apparently decided the effort was not worth the gain. The camp's reading campaign ended. Jerry slept that night grateful his resistance had spared other men.

The year 1969 began with the brief reading campaign and gambling. The Alcatraz POWs wagered who could pick the date of their homecoming. They aggressively placed bets, payable upon homecoming in food or cash as usual. Optimist Jim Mulligan predicted their release as June 1969—six months distant. Jerry joined him with a sunny bet. Other rosy predictions tapped down the cellblock. Then Stockdale placed his bet from across the courtyard. It landed like a bomb: February 1973. The prediction shocked Jerry. He couldn't fathom his country leaving POWs in Hanoi for four more years. Besides, he couldn't *survive* four more years.

"After the next [presidential] election," Stockdale tapped pessimistically. "Then we'll be going home and not before then." With no other choice, the POWs settled in to learn who would win the bet. Jerry felt certain it would not be Jim Stockdale. Surely, the new man in the White House, Richard Nixon, would bring them home soon.

A terrible scream knifed through the predawn quiet on January 23, 1969, three days after Hanoi Hannah reported Nixon's inauguration. The cry immediately awoke Jerry and every other POW in Alcatraz; the slightest abnormal noise in the courtyard would often rouse every man. Jerry thought it odd that despite being locked safely inside a cell, his body processed even the smallest noises as if they might signal some dire threat. He heard more screaming. "J" came down the wall: Harry Jenkins was having terrible cramps.

"Báo cáo, báo cáo!" cried Jenkins, in between screams. Other POWs joined Jenkins in calling the guards: "Báo cáo!" Jerry heard a commotion as several guards entered the camp. A cell door opened and the screaming subsided. Then he heard Jenkins bellow, "Go ahead, hit me!" Jerry assumed the guards were beating Jenkins to stifle his screams. Jerry and other POWs began pounding on their doors and yelling through their open vents in protest. Their chorus grew. Jerry felt a swelling pride. He and his men were standing up for a brother POW in need. He felt even better when guards walked down the cellblock, promising the inmates Jenkins would see a doctor.

Jim Stockdale assumed the worst; he believed the guards had beaten an ill prisoner. He declared a two-day hunger strike as retaliation. On January 24, Jerry and every other POW refused to eat. The next morning, Stockdale simply vanished. Nobody saw him leave and nobody knew his fate. Speculation abounded. Jerry suspected the North Vietnamese blamed Stockdale for the Alcatraz Gang's protest on behalf of Harry Jenkins, but all Jerry knew for sure was that full command now fell to him. He shouldered responsibility for the lives of the remaining nine men, ten including himself. It became his job to lead them home safely. With so little control over circumstances, he felt like history's weakest leader.

Shortly after the POWs realized the Camp Authority had removed Stockdale, a guard opened Jerry's cell door. Jerry's eyes adjusted to the light outside, and he saw that two civilians accompanied the guard. Obviously concerned about the hunger strike, the guard asked about the POWs' refusal to eat. Jerry immediately complained that guards had beaten an ill Harry Jenkins and the POWs were protesting. "There has been a misunderstanding," the guard said. "We will prove to you that you will get humane treatment when you are sick."

The guard introduced one of the civilians as a physician. The man entered Jerry's cell and conducted a physical. Jerry was surprised by its thoroughness and the doctor's kindness. When he left, he gave Jerry medicine to heal several cuts, rid him of intestinal worms, and clear up a bad rash he'd developed. According to the cellblock walls, the doctor treated every man in Alcatraz.

"They gave up," someone tapped out. "We won."

"Let's eat," tapped another. The men were ready to end Stockdale's hunger strike.

In cell 10, Jerry Denton had other plans. Stockdale had ordered a forty-eight-hour strike; just over twenty-four had passed. When Jerry scrubbed down the latrine area, he broadcast, "My order is steady as she goes." He heard immediate responses: groans and shouts. On the wall, POWs tapped out the case for lifting the hunger strike. Jerry needed to respect Stockdale's initial order; he also knew the men needed food badly. Realistically, he also faced a unified and boisterous opposition. Sometimes, he decided, leadership means compromise. When afternoon mealtime came, Jerry tapped out, "Eat."

Once Stockdale left, the Camp Authority again launched a campaign to squeeze letters of apology out of the POWs. Every man in Alcatraz felt the burn of ropes and the pain of various forms of duress. Some remained on their knees on hard concrete. Others were beaten with fan belts or worked over with ropes. While recovering from his own bout with ropes and fists, Jerry Denton heard a group of female soldiers viciously assail Sam Johnson in a neighboring quiz room. They literally beat him into submission.

Mickey Mouse made him sign a letter of apology, and Sam cried on the floor after the Mouse left. "What have I done," he wondered aloud. "I gave in too easily. I should have held out longer . . ."

Jerry heard him and called out, "Sam, it's okay buddy."

"I made them write it, Jerry," Sam whispered back. "But I had to sign it."

"It's okay, Sam," Jerry reassured him. "You're okay. Hang on. You did good."

The men did their best during that brutal period, but they all lost. They all signed the apologies, the confessions. They all sought forgiveness from one another and always received it. "GBU" was never tapped out with more understanding or sincerity than during the winter and spring of 1969 in Alcatraz.

Thankful they all had lived to see Easter, Jerry composed another poem for the 1969 holiday. He entitled it "La Pieta," after Michelangelo's 1499 sculpture of Mary holding a crucified Jesus.

La Pieta

The soldiers stare, then drift away,
Young John finds nothing he can say,
The veil is rent; the deed is done;
And Mary holds her only son.

His limbs grow stiff, the night grows cold,
But naught can loose that mother's hold,
Her gentle, anguished eyes seem blind,
Who knows what thoughts run through her mind?

Perhaps she thinks of last week's palms,
With cheering thousands off'ring alms
Or dreams of Canaan on the day
She nagged him till she got her way.

HER FACE SHOWS GRIEF BUT NOT DESPAIR,
HER HEAD THOUGH BOWED HAS FAITH TO SPARE,
FOR EVEN NOW SHE COULD SUPPOSE
HIS THORNS MIGHT SOMEHOW YIELD A ROSE.

HER LIFE WITH HIM WAS FULL OF SIGNS
THAT GOD WRITES STRAIGHT WITH CROOKED LINES.
DARK CLOUDS CAN HIDE THE RISING SUN,
AND ALL SEEM LOST, WHEN ALL BE WON!

Jerry laboriously tapped out the poem on the wall, sending its earnest words to fellow POWs. Words of thanks returned. Reading between his lines, someone named him the president of the Optimist Club. At heart, the Alcatraz Gang fervently hoped their own crooked lines were part of God's mysterious plan.

———

Late one night in May 1969, Jerry stirred. Someone was grabbing him, rocking him awake. Jerry opened his eyes and saw Mickey Mouse in the dim light. Jerry looked around dazedly and guessed the hour had passed 2:00 a.m. What on earth did Mickey Mouse want?

"Denton," Mickey Mouse said urgently, "I have something to tell you. I know you usually don't believe me, but time will prove I am telling the truth. I have just come from a meeting at headquarters. I have received information to make provisions for *two* more years."

Jerry struggled to digest the commandant's news.

"I must provide for *two* more Christmases," Mickey Mouse reiterated, holding up two fingers. Jerry was dumbfounded. He'd sensed they were nearing the end of this nightmare. Now, it would continue through Christmas 1970 at least. That would be *at least* five and a half years of his life devoured by Hanoi. At a minimum, two more years would pass before he saw his family. How could *this* be God's plan? Mickey Mouse might as well have awakened him with a baseball bat.

Dejected, Jerry spent the night dwelling on his darkening prospects. He gave himself a one-in-four chance of going home alive. He gave himself a one-in-fifty chance of emerging with his sanity. Perhaps, Jerry mused, the extended sentence might lead the Camp Authority to ease off the torture regime. It didn't.

———

From across the courtyard, Jim Mulligan began to pass Jerry worrisome news about Ron Storz, perhaps the most fanatical resister among the POWs. Unlike Mulligan, Jerry, and others, Storz had difficulty boxing away home. He dwelled on his wife and two young children throughout the day. He could not put those memories aside and focus on the present. Depression settled heavily on Ron Storz and cell 5. He stopped eating. In late May, Jerry learned that Storz had passed out in his cell and guards had removed him from Alcatraz. Rumors spread that Ron had hurt himself. Soon, Mulligan flashed that Mickey Mouse was keeping

Storz just across an alleyway from camp and providing care. Mulligan had seen Storz briefly and Ron had whispered, "There's no way the war's going to end soon. We'll be here forever." Mulligan observed Storz's withered frame and ordered him to eat.

As summer 1969 wore on, Ron Storz recovered enough to walk into the courtyard and empty his own latrine bucket. Jerry inhabited the closest cell to the latrine, so he did his best to communicate. He found Ron's mental state declining; he often appeared irrational. Jerry communicated to Ron that he could accept early release if he felt his life was in danger. Jerry sensed this might well be the case. He hoped Ron could save himself from his mental decline. Jerry saw that solitary confinement at Alcatraz was making his friend lose his mind. But Ron didn't accept any offers to leave early.

Jerry eventually learned Slick had returned and replaced the more ruthless Mickey Mouse as commandant at Alcatraz. He had given Ron playing cards and was teaching him to play bridge. Jerry hoped Slick's bridge lessons might improve Ron's state of mind. To encourage him, Jerry wrote a three-page note about rules and bidding. He left it hidden at the latrine. On Ron's every visit, he'd scrape or whisper questions about the game and Jerry would respond. One day, Jerry didn't answer quickly enough and Storz blurted, "Well, I know who my *real* friends are!" Jerry spent hours worrying about this weakening member of their band and how he could get him home.

Time in solitary took its toll on all the POWs in Alcatraz. Fraying nerves and desperation led some toward depression and others toward irrationality. Jerry observed it via taps through the wall, but he didn't always see it in himself. One warm summer evening, a guard stopped outside Jerry's door and stated the POWs needed to prepare for a move. Jerry demanded to see the officer in charge. Slick came to the courtyard and explained the Red River might flood. The Camp Authority wanted to ensure the safety of the POWs and move them. Jerry didn't believe him. "We're going home and they won't tell us the truth," Jerry tapped excitedly after Slick left. McKnight passed his message along the chain. A response from Bob Shumaker came back: "You're optimistic enough to buy the Brooklyn Bridge."

He was, he knew it, and by God, he'd be vindicated! Too excited to tap softly, Jerry began pounding out naval orders for getting a ship under way. He finished with "Anchors aweigh!" His figurative vessel didn't move. Jerry sat on his bedroll for hours. After midnight, Slick returned and announced there would be no move. POWs should sleep. Jerry sent a self-effacing message to Shumaker: "My anchor got fouled in the Brooklyn Bridge."

In September 1969, Hanoi Hannah announced that Hồ Chí Minh was ill. "The very best medical care is being given to our beloved leader," her voice told the POWs in Alcatraz. "All Vietnam's medical expertise is available to him. We are confident of his recovery."

"Yeah right," Sam Johnson tapped. "We know what North Vietnam's best medical care is all about."

"He's a dead man," panned Shumaker.

On September 2, Vietnam's Independence Day, Hanoi Hannah confirmed North Vietnam's leader had died at age seventy-nine. For a time, the POWs seemed forgotten as the Camp Authority mourned Hồ Chí Minh, the man who had freed them from French colonialism, and would, as they often told the POWs, expel the Americans and reunify Vietnam.

Unbeknownst to Jerry and the other POWs, North Vietnam's new leader, Lê Duẩn, soon issued an important directive that likely saved many long-suffering Americans. The new policy stated, "Although we do not consider the enemy pilots to be prisoners of war, bound by the 1949 Geneva Convention on the treatment of POWs, we still apply the principles of this convention in our humanitarian policy." The resolution provided for prisoners' health, living conditions, and right to worship. It allowed POWs to send one postcard home each month; they could receive one package every two months. It also stated, "From now until 1970, [we will] gradually allow the American enemy pilots that we are holding in secret to contact their families via postcards."

Also unbeknownst to Jerry was that his wife, Jane, and hundreds of other wives and family members of men declared prisoners of war or missing in action had become the imprisoned Americans' greatest advocates. These women had unified a polarized America and rallied it around one common cry: *Don't forget the POWs.* The National League of POW-MIA Families had lobbied so hard and loudly that they effectively changed United States policy on POWs in North Vietnam. Under Lyndon

Johnson, the government declined to criticize Hanoi for its refusal to honor the Geneva Convention, including its refusal to release the names of captured POWs, refusal to allow inspections of POW camps, and its illegal and inhumane treatment of American POWs. The Johnson administration feared that publicly disclosing such behavior would jeopardize peace negotiations. The increasingly vocal wives and their League drove the Nixon administration to change course. On the day of Nixon's inauguration, the new president received more than two thousand telegrams about the POW-MIA issue. Not coincidentally, in May 1969, new secretary of defense Melvin Laird publicly condemned North Vietnam's treatment of prisoners. The resulting negative publicity and international pressure drove Hanoi to change its policy in camps across North Vietnam, including Alcatraz. The change came just in time for many POWs who were barely surviving.

Jerry and his compatriots didn't know about these underlying forces or new policies per se, but they soon reaped the benefits. That fall, a guard caught Jerry communicating, and Slick called him to quiz. "Denton, you have been caught communicating," he said. "You know what has happened before."

"Yes, sir," Jerry answered. Did Slick have more punishment in store? Another confession or plea for amnesty?

"I am going to surprise," Slick replied giddily. "This time you will not be punish. We still have regulation and you have broken it, and I will criticize you for it. But as long as I am in authority, there will be no more punishment for communicating."

THE POW-MIA MOVEMENT

WHEN A NAVAL OFFICER informed Jane Denton that her husband, Jerry, had been shot down over North Vietnam, he offered condolences, then instructed her to "keep quiet." Any comments she made about her husband's status as missing in action (MIA) or as prisoner of war (POW) might endanger him and adversely affect potential peace negotiations with North Vietnam. Hundreds of other POW-MIA families received the same bizarre warning.

Months and years passed. Families received little, if any, word from Vietnam. The US government made no progress toward winning the release of POWs or improving their plight, yet the gag rule remained in effect. Families grew ever more frustrated and angry, especially as reports of prisoner maltreatment surfaced.

Jane Denton, along with other POW-MIA wives like Sybil Stockdale and Louise Mulligan, began meeting together and sharing their common nightmare. Were their husbands still alive? How were they being treated? Was their government ever going to bring them home?

Frustrated POW-MIA families banded together and, in 1968, boldly broke the "keep quiet" policy. They became vocal advocates for their loved ones. The US government stood by as the National League of POW-MIA Families launched a nationwide advocacy campaign for American servicemen listed as captured or missing in Vietnam. In 1969, they pressed the administration of new president

171

Richard Nixon so hard that his defense secretary changed national policy and publicly criticized North Vietnam for its violation of the Geneva Convention.

The League created two powerful symbols of their cause: first, a black-and-white flag featuring the silhouette of a POW, and second, the motto "You are not forgotten." The image quickly became ubiquitous, and their flag still flies today.

The League also leveraged metal POW-MIA bracelets to raise awareness in a uniquely personal way. More than five million Americans wore polished wristbands inscribed with the name of a missing or captured serviceman. These became the first cause-related wristbands.

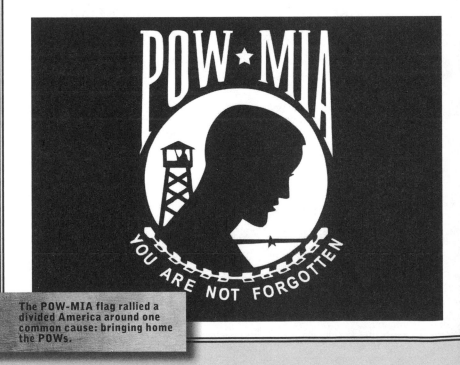

The POW-MIA flag rallied a divided America around one common cause: bringing home the POWs.

With their iconic symbols and heartfelt advocacy, this band of family-members-turned-activists united a bitterly polarized nation around American servicemen captured in Vietnam. Theirs became one of history's most extraordinary women's movements.

More than five million Americans wore metal wristbands to show support for missing and imprisoned servicemembers in Vietnam.

Jerry barely stopped himself from crying in front of Slick. He couldn't help but feel grateful to his adversary. For the first time in many months, he felt hopeful. Maybe he'd survived the worst. Perhaps it would finally get better. He knew many POWs could not persevere much longer under such harsh conditions.

The same guard caught Jerry communicating the next day. Slick called him to quiz. "Ah, Denton, you did it again," the commandant said. "The guard is doing his duty, but you will not be punished." Jerry let himself believe change—albeit small change—had come.

Bananas and vitamins soon appeared with breakfast, along with sugar and bread. Guards allowed POWs more time outside; they could walk freely about the Alcatraz courtyard for fifteen or thirty minutes at a time. They sometimes allowed Jerry to leave his door open. On one October day, Jim Mulligan appeared. "Hi, Jerry," he said.

Jerry replied, "Hi, Jim." They hadn't seen each other face-to-face since the summer of 1967. A guard gently ushered Mulligan back to his cell. Yes, change had come. Perhaps the Camp Authority planned to return the POWs to America soon.

The new understanding warmed the relationship between commanding officers—Slick and Jerry. They staged ideological discussions with each other during which Slick recounted the history of North Vietnam. He pointed out that by siding with French colonialism, Western nations had pushed Hồ Chí Minh toward Communist neighbors, China and the Soviet Union. Vietnam was not beholden to China or the Soviet Union; those alliances were of convenience or necessity. Hồ Chí Minh had been a nationalist foremost. Jerry understood.

"He went to Russia for help when he believed no one else would help him to obtain freedom for his country," Jerry conceded. Then Jerry explained how America had needed France's support to contain the Soviet Union in Europe after World War II and had thus supported France's reassertion of control over Vietnam. Slick felt America never comprehended the historical complexities and modern realities of Vietnam. Siding with an unpopular and undemocratic monarch in South Vietnam proved that.

Jerry wasn't prepared to defend or fully explain the long string of decisions by Presidents Truman, Eisenhower, Kennedy, Johnson, and Nixon that had led to the present situation. He shifted back to the philosophical, where he perceived he had the advantage. He said, "What I can't understand is the Communist suppression of political, religious, and press freedoms."

"Denton, you have seen more and read more, and you know more than I do," Slick responded. "You can make argument that I cannot answer. But you must understand we never have security. We always fight. We have no unity. Under French there was no security, no law for Vietnamese. If Vietnamese woman raped, or peasant murdered by French, there would be nothing that could happen to those that did it. We had nothing but corruption. Now for the first time we have security. We do not have other things, but for the first time we have precious security."

Jerry saw tears in Slick's eyes. He gripped Jerry's forearm and asked, "Do you understand that?"

Slick's statement reminded Jerry that every side has a story. But since the Camp Authority still confined Jerry and his men to claustrophobic four-by-ten-foot cells, his sympathy extended only so far.

Even with the improved treatment, Ron Storz's decline continued. Jerry assessed his condition each day, peering from beneath his door as Storz visited the latrine. Jerry constantly ordered him to eat. Storz claimed he'd resumed eating, but Jim Mulligan reported differently. Mulligan flashed that he'd gone to empty Storz's bucket and found the previous day's rations undisturbed. The POWs did not know how to help their friend.

One early December day, Jerry watched Ron Storz walk to the latrine. "You're all moving out of here," Storz said loudly. "The guards told me they are sending you out. But I'm not going."

Damned if Jerry would leave without one of his men. "Of course you're coming with us," Jerry retorted. "We're not letting you stay here by yourself."

"It will only be worse if I leave," Storz replied. "Besides, it's all a bluff. It's a trick to try and get me to eat, but I'm on to them. If they do move us, they will never let me be with you. They'll separate us."

"That won't happen, Ron," Sam Johnson said through his transom. "Things have changed some. Can't you feel that it's different now? We'll all be together."

At his next quiz with Slick, Jerry demanded, "If we are going to move, you must make Storz go with us."

"You are not going to move," Slick answered. "No need to worry about it."

Jerry didn't let the subject go. He revisited the subject just days later and got a different response. "You may move," Slick said. "It is not certain. But your Storz may do as he likes."

On December 9, 1969, a guard opened Jerry's cell door. He ordered Jerry to collect his belongings, and for what Jerry hoped would be the last time, he stepped out of his cell at Alcatraz. Hopes of homecoming rose in Jerry yet again. Could this be the end? *Yes,* Jerry decided as he walked toward the courtyard's exit, *we aren't just leaving Alcatraz, we are finally going home!* As the guard led him out of the courtyard and toward a waiting truck, he saw Slick approaching. "Ah, Denton," he said, "this time you will not ride in handcuffs. We will blindfold, but you will not be uncomfortable."

Before he could respond to Slick, someone covered his eyes and tightened a blindfold. Hands pushed him into the truck with several other POWs. Jerry didn't need wheels to carry him through Hanoi—he could have floated. He'd be home for Christmas.

Chapter 12

CAMP UNITY

JERRY SAT ALONE IN STARDUST, back in Hỏa Lò Prison, dejected but thinking his new cell seemed like a presidential suite compared to Alcatraz. He listened to guards manhandling Jim Mulligan into a nearby cell. "You bastards!" bellowed his friend. "You can't do this to me. I'm supposed to be going home!" How could they have been so naïve? How could they have let themselves believe homecoming had arrived? Leaving Alcatraz, Jerry had been elated. But when the truck had slowed down after ten minutes, turned, and entered a familiar-sounding tunnel, he knew it had not arrived at the airport. Instead, the Alcatraz Gang had returned to the Hanoi Hilton.

Activity in the Stardust cellblock subsided and Jerry heard the last guard leave. Jerry coughed out D for Denton. He heard H, J, M, T, R, and L come echoing back: Rutledge, Jenkins, Mulligan, Tanner, Shumaker, and Johnson.

Someone whispered, "Where are Coker and McKnight?"

Another responded, "They rode over with us from Alcatraz, so they must be here somewhere."

"What about Ron?" another POW asked. The men began shouting, "Ron!"

The noise attracted guards, who entered the cellblock yelling, "Shut up! Shut mouth! No talk!" The chatter ceased and the POWs quietly contemplated their poor fortune and their dim prospects until they fell sleep.

The next morning, a guard opened Jerry's door and indicated he'd take Jerry to wash. Jerry walked into the Little Vegas courtyard. He wore ragged shorts and carried a thin towel, sliver of soap, and bucket. He coughed out his initials. He wanted all POWs to know he had returned after twenty-five months of exile. He encountered Cat before reaching the bathhouse.

"Ah, Denton, I believe," Cat said and extended his hand.

"Yes, Denton," Jerry replied with some irritation. Cat knew exactly who he was.

"Long time since I see you, Denton."

"Yes, not since the banana and the torture," Jerry shot back and continued on to the bath.

The next day, Cat called Jerry to his office. With a solemn face, he said, "I have some very important announcements, Denton. I, other officers, and many of the guards had in our rage allowed ourselves to vent our anger on the prisoners and were responsible for deviations from our Vietnamese tradition of humane treatment. I have been required to make public self-criticism for my mistakes and from now on you will be allowed to follow the Code of Conduct."

Cat's statement shocked Jerry. He'd *admitted* the Camp Authority had tortured the POWs. He'd almost apologized.

Cat continued, "I will prove by my deeds that my words are true, and I want ideas from you on how we can apply humane treatment, including games and movies. We shall have many discussions in the future. Here are French-Vietnamese and English-French dictionaries for consultation to make sure we understand each other."

Floored, Jerry watched Cat walk away. He surmised that North Vietnam feared President Richard Nixon would escalate the war until America won, and Hanoi did not want to be held accountable for crimes committed against POWs. Cat had perhaps become a scapegoat. In his next meetings with Cat, Jerry demanded everyone receive a roommate; solitary confinement must end. He stipulated several other conditions under the Code. Cat generally agreed. When Jerry asked about the whereabouts of Jim Stockdale, however, Cat said nothing more than "Stockdale is tranquil." He said nothing about Ron Storz. Jerry feared for his fellow leader and for the young resister.

After several days back in the Hanoi Hilton, Jerry learned that Coker and McKnight were in the Mint. Nobody had seen Ron Storz. Jerry also discovered that in his absence the American resistance had indeed faltered. Some POWs had yet to join the communication network. Others had cooperated with the Camp

Authority without being tortured. Some freely read on the radio, something that gave the Alcatraz POWs fits.

Jerry took control and reasserted discipline among the American prisoners. He whispered over shower stalls, dropped notes in the courtyard, and tapped out lengthy messages to let POWs know torture had ended; they needn't fear the Camp Authority anymore. They should say no. They should stop cooperating. Other Alcatraz veterans shared the same messages wherever they went. Jerry issued orders to a renegade group of POWs in the Desert Inn cellblock to stop reading on the radio and writing for the camp magazine. When he received no response, he shouted out their names and demanded they stop. He observed them regularly eating outside, a special privilege afforded nobody else. He complained to Cat, who stonewalled him. "I am your uncle," Cat said. "I have good nephews and bad nephews. I shall treat some better than others, but all will be treated well."

On December 23, 1969, the door of Jerry's Stardust cell opened. Jim Mulligan walked in, carrying his gear. The two commanders looked at each other until the guard closed the door. Then they embraced. Joyful, they slapped each other on the back and broke into cheek-hurting smiles. Both men had endured more than two years of solitary confinement since their last stint together in 1967—more than 780 days, 18,720 hours, or 1,123,200 minutes alone. Add to that Jerry's 738 days alone prior to Alcatraz. They marveled they weren't utterly crazy.

On Christmas Day, the reunited roommates walked through an unusually active camp to the game room. They found a Christmas tree and nativity scene, along with other decorations. The scene dumbfounded them. They were sure the Camp Authority planned a propaganda stunt, but when guards began bringing full cups of steaming coffee, they decided to play along. Jerry relished the strong French roast, sweet with sugar.

Cat himself arrived next, in his pressed khaki uniform. He retrieved two plates laden with food. "Eat, Denton. Eat, Mulligan," he said, delivering the hot meals. The POWs bowed and said, "Thank you, Commander." They cleaned their plates of carrots, potatoes, cabbage, and turkey.

Christmas continued as Cat distributed letters from home, along with photographs and packages. Jerry knew the Camp Authority had kept these from him for years or months. Nevertheless, he had them now and felt fortunate. He gazed at the letters and photographs for the remainder of the afternoon. He saw a growing family that had changed noticeably from the one he left in 1965. In particular, and not happily, he noticed his sons' hair getting longer. In wrapped packages, Jane had sent coffee, protein pills, soap, and chocolate drink mix. It was the first care package Jerry had received; surely the worst was over.

The year 1970 began with Jerry and the Alcatraz Gang restoring order to Little Vegas and the Hanoi Hilton. They wrote signs saying "Don't read" on toilet paper and held them up in their windows when POWs who were still operating outside the Code of Conduct came into the courtyard. Jerry did not relent and soon Little Vegas was, for the most part, aligned and running like a military unit under his command.

His last major gripe involved Sam Johnson, the one POW still in solitary. Jerry complained to Cat. "Ah, Denton," Cat said. "Johnson is a bad nephew. He will never have a roommate." Jerry relayed the bad news to Sam. "Don't worry, Sam," he said. "We'll think of something." He remembered the signs of depression and madness he'd seen in Ron Storz. He began seeing the same dangerous indicators in Sam Johnson. On April 30, Jerry ordered a hunger strike to protest Sam's solitary confinement. He and most POWs in Little Vegas refused to eat unless Sam received a cellmate. The fast infuriated Cat, but he did not relent. It lasted for three days, until Jerry felt POWs were jeopardizing their own health. Jerry ordered half rations until May 11. Nothing had changed for Sam, however, and the POWs had to give up the effort. Sam continued his own personal hunger strike. Jerry learned he'd collapsed in the game room while playing pool alone; he was starving himself. Jerry got on the wall: "Sam, I'm giving you a direct order. Stop the fast. Don't hurt yourself."

At last, Cat told Jerry he'd let Sam visit him and Mulligan. "Sam," Jerry whispered across the corridor when he'd returned to his cell, "Cat told me you are going to be allowed to visit with Mulligan and me. Try to act surprised when they come to get you or they'll know we've been communicating and they'll call off the visit."

Several days later, the door to Jerry and Jim Mulligan's cell opened. There stood Sam Johnson. He looked like a skeleton. He stood at attention and said, "Major Sam Johnson reporting, sir." Jerry grabbed him in a bear hug as Sam's whole body sobbed. Tears traced down the cheeks of each man. Sam began daily visits, and Cat soon moved him into a cell with Bob Shumaker and Nels Tanner. Johnson knew Shumaker well; the navy whiz had taught Johnson French through their shared wall at Alcatraz.

Two months later, Jerry heard movement outside his door. He heard muffled voices in the neighboring cell. Then taps came through the wall from Johnson: He'd just been moved into a cell with Jim Stockdale. All of Stardust celebrated Stockdale's reemergence. He'd been lost for a year and a half, since January 1969. The Alcatraz Gang had reassembled, with the exception of Ron Storz. They had heard nothing from or about Ron in nearly a year; they feared he hadn't survived. Sam reported that Stockdale had barely survived his own ordeal. He'd been sequestered and tortured in the Hanoi Hilton since leaving Alcatraz. The experience left him badly addled.

The POW experience seemed to have affected Cat too. Jerry had noticed a gradual change in his adversary during the spring and summer of 1970. He'd lost a star of rank on his collar, and he seemed increasingly humble. His arrogance had vanished; a tic developed above one eye. Once lord of the prison system, Cat now seemed a fallen figure. He made fewer and fewer appearances. Neither Jerry nor any other POW saw Cat again after mid-1970.

Jerry Denton passed command to Jim Stockdale on November 1, 1970, once the grizzled leader had sufficiently recovered. Several weeks later, Colonel Robbie Risner arrived at the Hanoi Hilton, having emerged from a long isolation, and took over from Stockdale. Then two more senior officers transferred in and took command, one after the other. Jerry wondered what caused the influx of POWs from other camps into the Hilton.

In fact, a daring American raid on the POW camp in the Hanoi suburb of Sơn Tây sparked the change. While navy and air force aircraft staged a distraction over the North Vietnamese coastline, helicopters carrying fifty-six US Army Special Forces Green Berets snuck across North Vietnam's western border on November 21, 1970. They skimmed trees and fields on their way

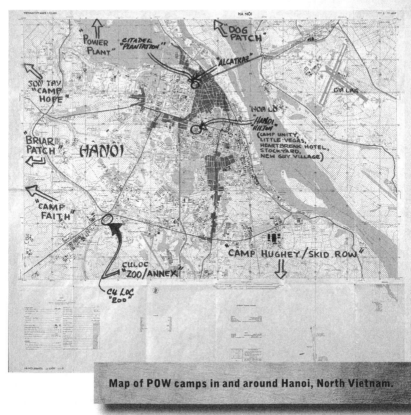

Map of POW camps in and around Hanoi, North Vietnam.

185

to Sơn Tây. US intelligence had reported numerous American POWs in the camp there, and the army trained exceptionally hard for this rescue mission. Unfortunately, the intelligence was out of date. The Camp Authority had transferred the POWs out of the camp four months earlier. The raiders landed inside the prison compound to find empty cells and few North Vietnamese troops. They returned to Thailand safely but empty-handed. The daring mission *did* convince the Camp Authority to consolidate their American prisoners in the Hanoi Hilton, however. The POWs finally learned of the raid from a roll of microfilm smuggled inside a care package received in late 1971. But during 1970, many were wondering if their country had forgotten them.

———

Jerry and Jim Mulligan spent December 23, 1970, plucking feathers and cleaning turkeys for a Christmas meal for the eighty men in the Little Vegas section of the Hanoi Hilton. Jerry pulled feathers one at a time, thinking *She loves me, she loves me not*, with every two plucks. They worked so slowly, Camp Authority staff finished the job themselves. Back in their cell, Jerry contemplated how many more Christmases he'd spend in North Vietnam. The coming Christmas would be his sixth.

On Christmas Eve, Jerry and Jim Mulligan lay on their bunks talking. They counted down the moments until an evening bell marked the end of another day in Hanoi. For Jerry, this evening's bell would mark 1,986 days.

They suddenly heard movement in the courtyard. Jerry pulled himself up to the window. "It must be some sort of move, Jim," he said. "I can see the water girls and cooks moving dishes from the main area and taking them out of the main entrance toward Heartbreak Hotel." Taps came that another cellblock was moved out. Then Jerry saw guards empty two more buildings. Eventually, the Alcatraz veterans in Stardust seemed to be the last POWs in Little Vegas. As Jerry wondered if they were beginning another sequestration, he heard noise in the corridor. A guard loudly ordered the POWs to roll their gear into their mats. He unlocked their cells and organized the men in a single-file line. Jerry trudged out of Stardust and into the unknown yet again. This time, he wore no blindfold.

The Stardust inmates followed guards through the prison's main courtyard, past Heartbreak Hotel, and into a new sector. Jerry looked at a large, open yard surrounded by low cellblocks. Guards directed the Alcatraz men into the first building on the right. A large number 7 marked the door. Jerry stepped into a lighted room with nearly fifty other Americans, all unbound and unfettered. He had not seen this many Americans together since the dreadful march through downtown Hanoi in 1966. Every man inside was overjoyed.

Embraces, smiles, and stories filled the next hour inside Room Seven. Jerry watched his fellow POWs reunite with old squadron mates; he finally saw the faces of many POWs with whom he'd communicated blindly during his solitary days. POWs rarely saw the face on the other side of the wall. The men now passed information freely: where they'd been, whom they'd seen, what they'd endured. Happily, Jerry learned his right-seater, Bill Tschudy, was alive and well.

Talk eventually quieted and Jerry spoke up. "Hey, it's practically Christmas," he said. "Why don't we have a church service?"

Several POWs volunteered to help. Jerry turned to his favorite Texan, Sam Johnson. "And Sam will sing, won't you, Sam?"

"Shirley won't even let me sing in church when there are other voices to cover me up," Sam protested.

"It doesn't matter," said Jerry. "Just sing a Christmas carol."

Sam's breaking voice sang the first line of "Silent Night." Jerry and the other POWs joined him. In the dark of Hanoi, the men's rising voices offered long-awaited light. Jerry savored a rare peace.

The Camp Authority was having none of it, however. Guards rushed in, demanding the Americans stop singing: "No authorize! No authorize! Be quiet!" An officer entered with the camp rules, pointed to regulations about prisoner gatherings, and stated, "Not allowed." Thus ended Christmas 1970.

The POWs let just two months pass before they again tested their captors. Jerry Denton and other leaders authorized a church service in Room Seven on Sunday, February 7, 1971. Worship began with hymns from a POW choir and ended with a homily and benediction. Just as congregants were being dismissed, Jerry saw three guards wade through the POWs and nab the minister and his officiants: George Coker, Howie Rutledge, and Robbie Risner. An officer berated them outside and began marching them away. That's when POWs began singing in protest.

Air force major Bud Day started off with "O say, can you see . . ." The rest of the room leapt in, ". . . by the dawn's early light?" Room Seven filled with booming voices as fifty Americans belted out "The Star-Spangled Banner." The singing spread to the other cellblocks in Camp Unity, as the POWs had named the area. By midsong, nearly four hundred POWs were singing in unison. The Church Riot of 1971 had begun.

Guards swarmed into the rooms, screaming, "No authorize! No authorize! Quiet! No singing!" The POWs just sang louder. The crescendo of the US national anthem echoed throughout the Hanoi Hilton; it flowed over the barbed wire and into the streets of the North Vietnamese capital. The imprisoned Americans were telling all of Hanoi that they had survived the worst; they would endure the rest.

Next, the prisoners belted out "God Bless America," then "Battle Hymn of the Republic," "America the Beautiful," "California, Here I Come," and "The Eyes of Texas." Jerry basked in the triumphant singing. His men, united in song, sang in proud defiance of their captors. Jerry felt happiness he'd not known for years. When the Camp Authority played its own music over the speakers, the men sang louder. They ran out of songs and switched to chanting. The boisterous men in Room Seven began, "This is Room Number Seven, Number Seven, Number Seven! This is Room Number Seven, where the hell is Six?" Room Six picked up the chant, passed it to Room Five. It circled the courtyard all the way to Room One. Only when troops with riot gear and tear gas entered Camp Unity did the Americans relent.

Once again, the Alcatraz Gang found itself at the center of trouble. Coker and Rutledge were sent to Heartbreak Hotel. The next day, Jerry and Jim Stockdale were sent to Building Zero and placed in stocks. Harry Jenkins and Jim Mulligan joined them within the week after sponsoring a raucous anniversary party for Bob Shumaker; February 11, 1971, marked six years in captivity for Shumaker. Robbie Risner was already in Building Zero, as was air force colonel John Flynn, the highest ranking officer in Hanoi. All the camp's senior officers were together. Flynn, Risner, Stockdale, and Denton ranked highest and became known as the Four Wise Men. From their confinements in Building Zero, they made Camp Unity a functioning air wing, issuing policies for the squadrons (rooms) and officers (POWs). They christened themselves the Fourth Allied POW Wing. "Fourth," since they fought in the fourth major conflict of the century. "Allied," as four Thai and South Vietnamese officers were among them.

Jerry considered South Vietnamese pilot Nguyễn Quốc Đạt—whom he and others called "Max"—a secret weapon for the Americans. Max and the Thai POWs, most importantly Thai special forces sergeant Chicharn Harnavee, received less scrutiny from camp guards. Some initially learned English via tap code and they all, at great risk, couriered notes, served as lookouts, and even shared new skills. Once, Max taught Jerry to fabricate black crayons from burnt bamboo and soap shavings. The Americans warmly welcomed these allies.

The remainder of 1971 passed slowly, as did much of 1972. Jerry appreciated not being tortured, yet nobody seemed to care what he did, period. He drifted toward purposelessness again. Issuing orders to men in cellblocks was no real leadership assignment. Yet regulations did remind the men they were still American officers, not criminals. They were still fighting a war, albeit in a most unexpected way. They should still aspire to return with honor.

To reclaim some meaning, the men organized a veritable university. Collectively, more than 350 POWs possessed an astounding amount of knowledge. Sam Johnson, a former Air Force Thunderbird aerobatic pilot, taught aerial maneuvers. Bob Shumaker taught French. Others taught auto mechanics, mathematics, engineering, literature, and philosophy. John McCain and Harry Jenkins were star movie-tellers; they'd perform entire movies from memory as evening entertainment. What they couldn't remember, they just improvised.

Packages arrived from home on a regular basis. The POWs thought they received about half the original contents; they often saw guards eating Planters peanuts or smoking American-brand cigarettes certainly meant for them. Jerry and Jim Mulligan opened one package together to find canned martinis. Mulligan also received a box of prunes. When he bit into one, he discovered a tiny plastic container hidden inside. He opened it and pulled out a roll of microfilm. None of the senior officers could read the tiny text, so they sent it to Room Seven, where Shumaker's and Coker's younger eyes were able to read a newspaper story about the Sơn Tây raid. The news caused celebration. They knew America had never forgotten them.

Hanoi Hannah continued to bring news of the outside world, complementing the news that POWs received via mail. When Jerry Denton had communicated with new shootdown Red McDaniel in 1967, Red reported America had nearly 500,000 troops in South Vietnam. By 1972, Hanoi Hannah reported America was deserting South Vietnam. President Nixon championed "peace with honor" and presided over a massive withdrawal that took four years. Troop levels fell to 156,000 in 1971 and 24,000 by late 1972. South Vietnam, which had seen four different undemocratic regimes since 1960, faced both internal and external challenges and increasingly had to fend for itself. With no clear path to victory, a weak and unsavory ally, and an electorate that had turned decidedly against the war, Nixon and the United States began putting Vietnam behind them. As America withdrew, Hannah reported Communist advances. Soon, she predicted, Saigon would be liberated and Vietnam reunited.

North Vietnam did not seem ready to negotiate. Heck, Jerry wouldn't negotiate either, were he in Hanoi's shoes. America seemed unwilling to force its enemy to the peace table. And if North Vietnam and their South Vietnamese allies, the Việt Cộng, were winning, why negotiate? The POWs prayed fervently that something would change, that America would force a treaty. If it didn't, they might remain in Camp Unity indefinitely.

Chapter 13

HOMECOMING

AFTER NIGHTFALL ON DECEMBER 18, 1972, Jerry felt the ground tremble. A low thunder rolled across Hanoi. Flecks of plaster floated down from the ceiling of his room. Jerry listened and realized it wasn't a heavy storm. "I think those are B-52s," he exclaimed as he hopped to the window. Sure enough, the rumbles and tremors continued; US Air Force strategic bombers were attacking Hanoi. Nixon had decided to force North Vietnam to negotiate! In Jerry's mind, homecoming suddenly became an undeniable possibility. POWs grasped the bars on their cells and looked skyward. They cheered as concussions rippled through the winter night and American airmen brought the war to North Vietnam's capital.

The raids continued relentlessly each night, pausing only for Christmas. They finally stopped on December 29. The evenings became silent once again. Jerry noticed radio tower lights now remained on throughout the night. A new oversized North Vietnamese flag flew over Hỏa Lò Prison. The guards seemed subdued. A strange quiet fell over Hanoi. The POWs speculated about what it meant. Had North Vietnam agreed to terms? When POWs arrived from recently downed B-52s, the pilots shared news that the war had neared an end. National Security Advisor Henry Kissinger had promised the country that "peace is at hand." If the bombing had stopped, North Vietnam had likely sued for peace. Hope ran high. In nobody did it run higher than in Jerry Denton.

On January 27, 1973, the Camp Authority assembled all the Americans in Camp Unity for the first time. Nearly four hundred members of history's longest-suffering military unit walked out of their rooms in shorts, pajamas, T-shirts, and boxers. All wore rubber flip-flops. They wore no shackles or blindfolds. No guards prodded them along with bayonets. They stood in formation and observed press and Camp Authority officials milling near the gates. Anticipation charged the air. The commandant of Hỏa Lò Prison walked before his prisoners. He stepped onto a small box and announced the war's end.

The POWs received the statement stoically, not entirely trusting the words and not wanting to show emotion before their captors and foreign journalists. The commandant continued and listed the treaty's conditions. At last, he confirmed a most important point. North Vietnam would release the prisoners, in groups of 120 men every two weeks, beginning February 12. Evacuation would proceed in order of shootdown, first to last.

Jerry digested the information; could this be the end, after so many years? His fellow POWs remained stone-faced. They too struggled with similar hopes and lingering suspicions. Yet today's announcement seemed sincere. Bombs no longer fell. Hanoi Hannah had been largely silent. The Camp Authority, at long last, seemed interested in the POWs' well-being. Jerry knew his optimism had spawned many false hopes. Today, he would let himself believe one last time.

Lieutenant Colonel Robbie Risner stood in front of the wing. Jerry watched him execute an about-face. "Fourth Allied POW Wing, atten-hut!" he barked. Sandals stamped on the dirt courtyard of Camp Unity as the Americans snapped to attention. Risner gave a salute. The leader of each cellblock returned it. Jerry saw pride on the faces of the fighting men standing alongside him in Hỏa Lò Prison. Their unexpected mission appeared almost complete. The cellblock leaders ordered, "Squadron, dis . . . *missed*!"

POWs walked about the courtyard, talking with one another. Then back in their rooms, they let themselves celebrate, away from the eyes of the press and Camp Authority. Jerry and the camp leadership hammered out an official statement and signaled to other rooms: "No celebrations, no fraternization or friendliness, and no unnecessary confrontation with the prison guards. All conduct will be dignified, professional, and on the guarded assumption that release is imminent. We will operate from a position of cautious optimism."

Things began to happen. The Camp Authority filled Rooms Four, Six, and Seven with 116 POWs captured before July 1966— the first men slated for release. Extra bread appeared with meals. POWs cooked for themselves in the courtyard; they filled up with vegetables and meats, wondering how they'd survived on thin phở for so long. Jerry's friend Bob Shumaker tracked prisoners' weight by dunking them in the courtyard's water tank. He'd calculate body mass by measuring cubic feet of water displaced and multiplying that figure by 62.4 pounds, the approximate weight of one cubic foot of water. Some men gained more than ten pounds while awaiting release.

The end of their imprisonment also brought sadness. The Alcatraz Gang learned for certain that Ron Storz had not survived. As they had feared, Ron never left Alcatraz. He'd died there in April of 1970.

In early February, Jerry squared off with Mickey Mouse for one last quiz. The former superintendent of Alcatraz asked what Jerry would say upon release. "I haven't answered your questions this long," Jerry responded. "Why should I answer you now? Why do you care what I say anyhow? There are hundreds of men who will speak when they get home."

"You have credibility, Denton."

"What do you expect? Don't you know I'll tell about the torture?"

"Yes, we expect that," Mickey Mouse said.

"Why do you want me to tell you what I will say?"

"We afraid when you get home and make a speech, Mr. Nixon will not give us aid he promised," explained Mickey Mouse. "Public would not allow."

"I will say that through 1969 you treated me and the others worse than animals," Jerry answered.

"Yes, but is that all?"

"No," said Jerry. "That is not all. Late in 1969 you came off the torture. After that, to my knowledge, you did not resort to extreme punishment. You then acted within your conscience, such as it is."

"That's the truth, but others may not tell the truth."

"If there is any exaggeration, the senior officers will take care of that," Jerry said.

As Jerry rose to leave, his longtime adversary stood with him. Mickey Mouse looked Jerry in the eye and said, "Denton, you're a good man."

Jerry awoke early on the morning of Monday, February 12, 1973. It was his 2,766th morning in North Vietnam; he expected it to be his last. Camp Unity bustled as guards delivered leather shoes, socks, khaki pants, button-down shirts, and jackets to the Americans. The Camp Authority had wanted to send the POWs home wearing sweaters or suits; the POWs had wanted to wear their pajamas. The khakis and shirts were a compromise, one of the few ever made with the POWs.

Jerry took one last cold shower, then donned real clothes for the first time in nearly eight years. He and other POWs wobbled as they readjusted to wearing shoes. Once dressed, POWs streamed out of their cellblocks and descended upon a rich breakfast of milk, bananas, bread, and coffee provided in the courtyard.

Soon, the 116 men to be released that day began to assemble; the rest would follow in the weeks to come.

Jerry organized the lucky men into two columns; Ev Alvarez and Bob Shumaker, the first two shootdowns, were at the head. Shumaker had spent exactly eight full years in captivity. Today was the first day of his ninth year; soon he'd see his son, now eight years and three months old. Jerry took his place in the column's seventh row next to his bombardier-navigator, Bill Tschudy.

Jerry looked over the group from front to back, eyeing men who'd been downed between August 1964 and July 1966. Together, they'd endured torture and deprivation, the "Make Your Choice" campaign, the Hanoi March, and the dreadful summer of 1967. A special handful had survived exile at Alcatraz. Jerry wondered if any other American unit had endured so much.

After a long hour of standing, Jerry received the order to mobilize. "Ev, we're going to march out in formation," Jerry called to Ev Alvarez at the column's head. "You count cadence." Jerry wanted his men to leave Hỏa Lò Prison like soldiers.

"Right face," Jerry ordered. "Count 'em off, Ev!"

Alvarez called, "Forward march!"

The disciplined column moved smartly toward the foreboding main gate through which so many POWs had entered captivity years ago, beaten, bloodied, and afraid. They passed through the dark tunnel and emerged onto the drizzly street. The column wheeled right before masses of quiet citizens who crowded the sidewalks. The last time Jerry had seen the local citizenry, they were attacking him during the POWs' ill-fated march through Hanoi during 1966. Now, they simply looked on curiously.

The Americans boarded waiting buses and rumbled through the battle-weary city. Jerry silently observed blocks of apartments and shops. People stopped to watch the three buses carrying men who'd spent up to eight years in their city. Once these men had been vilified daily. By February 1973, they had been largely forgotten.

Tears welled in Jerry's eyes as he thought about the hardship Hanoi's citizens would face rebuilding their country under a Communist regime. At least he could leave. Rabbit, Cat, and these men and women had to stay. The buses continued through light rain and across the Red River.

At Gia Lâm airport, the Americans waited in formation, looking at an empty airstrip and searching an overcast sky. Some grew nervous. Then POWs spied a silvery transport descending through the clouds, like an angel of deliverance. The men heard the whine of four jet engines. Soon they could read the words "US Air Force" emblazoned on the plane's side. The massive C-141 Starlifter landed gently, puffs of smoke issuing from its wheels. There would be no trickery or surprise. America had finally come.

The POWs advanced toward a tarp that shaded a delegation of North Vietnamese and American officials seated at a long table. Jerry spied Rabbit standing at a microphone. He called out the names of each POW, one by one. The twelfth name he called was Jeremiah Denton. Jerry stepped forward. He saw papers being signed at the official table. He shook the hand of a United States Air Force colonel. A uniformed escort walked him away from Rabbit, Hỏa Lò Prison, and nearly eight years of captivity. He walked toward freedom. He passed under the wing of the parked C-141, then climbed the ramp into the plane's cavernous belly. He joyfully embraced the eleven ex-POWs already aboard. Away from the eyes of captors and press, Jerry Denton celebrated.

Three planes would arrive that day to extricate American POWs from North Vietnam. When the first forty men had boarded Jerry's plane, the gate closed and the men buckled into their seats. The big plane taxied to the runway. Then the four engines roared as the pilot pushed the throttles forward. When the wheels left the ground, forty free men shouted at the tops of their lungs. It was 1:46 p.m., Monday, February 12, 1973.

———

Jerry was senior officer on the first flight, so he'd make the first public statement on behalf of the returning POWs. During the three-hour flight to Clark Air Base in the Philippines, he crafted what he'd say to the world. He knew cameras would carry his words to millions of viewers and, most importantly, to his wife, Jane, and their seven children. He shared a two-sentence statement with his fellow ex-POWs, or ex-cons as they were calling themselves in jest. They approved.

The passenger section of the C-141 offered no windows, so it wasn't until the plane landed in the Philippines and the door opened that Jerry saw the crowds. Hundreds had come to welcome the POWs back to American territory; their collective roar filled the aircraft. Jerry walked through the door and descended a short stairway. Wearing dark pants and a light Windbreaker, he saluted the commander of America's Pacific forces, who waited at the bottom of the stairs in his white navy uniform. Jerry turned toward the microphone and the cameras beyond. He blinked in the sunlight and began.

"We are honored to have had the opportunity to serve our country under difficult circumstances," he said. "We are profoundly grateful to our commander in chief and to our nation for this day."

Recently released prisoners of war on board the C-141 aircraft carrying them out of Hanoi to freedom on February 12, 1973.

He paused. He needed to say more. Heartfelt words welled up inside him. With his voice breaking, he concluded, "God bless America."

The crowd roared its approval. Jerry smiled humbly through moist eyes. He stepped forward to salute the American flag carried by the planeside color guard. He pivoted on his heel and marched down a red carpet to the buses that would whisk him and his men to the base hospital. From his seat, he watched his men file out of the C-141, one by one. They saluted the flag and strode, walked, limped, or hobbled down the ribbon of carpet. Despite nagging injuries, returning POWs made each step with pride. Neither Jerry nor any of his men had wished for such an assignment. None wished to spend the war in prison. None anticipated their mission would last so terribly long. But they had all done their duty as best they could, and they were going home.

The full buses drove through crowds chanting "Wel-come-home" and waving signs, banners, and flags. Shortly, the buses arrived at the Clark Air Base hospital. Jerry received a full physical. His doctor cleared him to eat, and he joined the flood of POWs converging on the cafeteria. Jerry saw men downing banana splits while in line for steak and eggs. He noticed cafeteria staff flash looks of disbelief as POWs piled plates with all the foods denied them in Hanoi. The men gorged themselves. Senior officers like Jerry joined right in. Next came hot showers; Jerry savored the steam and felt the water wash away years of grime and memories, both painful and proud.

Time came for Jerry to call home. An operator patched him through to Watergate Lane in Virginia Beach. He heard Jane's voice. It still dripped with Southern warmth and abiding love. It seemed as if no time had passed. They were as in love as ever. Jerry and Jane were lucky; many POWs received unsettling or tragic news on that first phone call home. Eight years brings many changes to families and relationships.

Grateful for his good fortune and exhausted from an emotional day, Jerry slipped between the crisp sheets of a soft hospital bed. He laid his head on a fresh down pillow and fell fast asleep. His dreams were those of a free man.

The US military's physicians weren't ready to declare him entirely free, however. Jerry's doctor explained that POWs needed further psychological evaluation before being released. The medical teams worried that after so long in captivity, POWs might be flat-out crazy. Jerry revolted. The only thing that would make him crazy was staying one more day in the hospital. The doctors relented. Jerry put himself on the first flight home. His old cellmate Jim Mulligan joined him for a nearly nine-thousand-mile journey home.

They were returning to a much-changed country, one needing closure after a decadelong war with few real victories. The United States had lost 58,000 sons and daughters in Vietnam; hundreds of thousands more suffered wounds both physical and emotional. Many returning troops never received thanks, appreciation, or even a simple "welcome home." An increasingly ugly and unpopular war had divided and disillusioned the public while fueling social upheaval. The citizenry had grown weary of stalemate and loss, of disheartening news from abroad. The return of POWs held in both North and South Vietnam gave the conflict a sorely needed final chapter. It gave the nation a common cause to celebrate. It allowed the country to unite and claim a victory at last. From coast to coast, jubilant Americans turned out to welcome home more than five hundred returning prisoners of war.

In the predawn hours of Thursday, February 15, 1973, Jerry Denton watched the twinkling lights of Norfolk and Virginia Beach shimmer below him. He saw swaths covered by the Chesapeake Bay and its tributaries. He tried to see the lights of Watergate Lane, where he'd bid Jane goodbye in May of 1965. He heard the airliner's engines change pitch, and the plane gently nosed toward Chambers Field at Naval Station Norfolk. The wheels touched down with a bump and the airliner taxied toward a wall of floodlights. The bright lights met Jerry and Jim Mulligan when they stepped out of the plane. Cheers washed over them. At Clark Air Base, they'd heard cheers from caring strangers. Now, they listened to the outpouring from dear family, friends, and colleagues who'd spent long years worrying and praying on their behalf. In a way, they had all brought Jerry Denton home.

Jerry walked down the stairs onto the tarmac, his head held high. He listened to the band. He absorbed the happy faces, the colorful banners, the American flags. He saw Jane and his family in the crowd. He wanted to rush straight to them, but he stepped to a microphone to perform his final duty. He thanked everyone for their love and for never forgetting the POWs. His words said, his mission ended at last. He stepped toward his family.

The eight of them met him with joyous hugs. He embraced Jane first. Then the children piled around him, each trying to wrap him in their arms, each trying to get close to their father. At times, each of them had doubted he'd ever return. Now, they could hold him, hear his laugh, and see his tears. His eldest son, Jerry III, was eighteen in 1965; his daughter Mary was age one. Now they were twenty-six and nine. To Jerry, Jane had never looked more beautiful.

Together, the family walked to the caravan that would take them to Portsmouth Naval Hospital, where they could visit away from the lights and media. There, Jerry would share a special, unique memory of each child that he'd treasured in Hanoi. Those memories, Jerry told his children, had seen him through his most difficult times. For a moment before the caravan left Naval Station Norfolk, Jerry and Jane had a car to themselves. Alone in the back seat, they held each other in an embrace for which both had waited nearly eight years.

Jerry Denton had kept his promise to Jane, his family, his men, and himself. He had returned with honor.

Jerry and Jane Denton reunited, February 15, 1973.
Jerry Denton had spent 2,766 days in captivity.

EPILOGUE

WHEN I FIRST MET JERRY DENTON at his Virginia home, I introduced myself and said, "Hello, Senator." He smiled and answered, "Alvin, I *was* a senator. I will always be an admiral."

To Jerry Denton, no other duty outranked his command in the prison camps of North Vietnam. Even the six years he served his home state of Alabama in the United States Senate did not compare. Never had he served with such devoted, duty-bound men as the members of the Fourth Allied POW Wing, and especially the brothers who carried one another through their ordeal in Alcatraz.

Jerry received his promotion to captain upon his release and his promotion to rear admiral shortly thereafter. He also received the Navy Cross for his leadership and heroism in Hanoi. He returned to duty not long after his homecoming. He continued serving in the navy until retiring in 1977. He mounted a successful US Senate campaign in 1980 and entered the Senate when Ronald Reagan entered the White House: January 1981. He remains the only navy admiral to serve in that body. The next year, 1982,

Surviving members of the Alcatraz Gang with their wives, 2001. From left: George McKnight, Sam Johnson, Nels Tanner, Jim Mulligan, Bob Shumaker, Jerry Denton, George Coker, Jim Stockdale.

President Reagan honored him in the annual State of the Union address. "We don't have to turn to our history books for heroes," said the fortieth president to his national audience. "They're all around us. One who sits among you here tonight epitomized that heroism at the end of the longest imprisonment ever inflicted on men of our armed forces. Who can ever forget that night when we waited for television to bring us the scene of that first plane landing at Clark Field in the Philippines—bringing our POWs home.

The plane door opened and Jeremiah Denton came slowly down the ramp. He caught sight of our flag, saluted, and said, 'God bless America,' then thanked *us* for bringing him home."

Jerry served one term in the Senate and narrowly lost reelection. Perhaps that was for the best. He brought to Washington an idealism that often clashed with the tactical and ever-political machinations of Capitol Hill. In 1987, he returned home to be with his family and devote time to the causes and people he held most dear—including his wife, Jane, who passed away in 2007. He and Jane had fourteen grandchildren.

———

On July 22, 2014, I sat in a hushed Old Post Chapel at Arlington National Cemetery alongside Jerry Denton's fellow Alcatraz prisoners US Congressman Sam Johnson, Admiral Bob Shumaker, Captain Jim Mulligan, and Commander George Coker. The flag-draped casket of Admiral Jeremiah A. Denton Jr. lay before us.

Jerry Denton III delivered a moving eulogy and recalled a line from my book *Defiant*. When the cards were down, I'd written, "Some POWs felt nobody but Jerry Denton had the guts to take over."

I thought how true that was. Jerry had guts. He defined leadership with a fearless sense of bold, almost unthinking self-sacrifice. In him, I met the rare individual who believes in duty. He went through the fire himself because his position, his code, and his oath all demanded it. He took the punches and the ropes first. If he didn't, how could he expect others to follow his orders?

The service ended with the singing of "God Bless America." I thought back to when Jerry Denton had first arrived in the Philippines and closed his brief remarks with those three words. By using them, he sparked a rebirth of the phrase. Still today, presidents, elected officials, and others often close their remarks with those words. It's important to remember that while their closings are often scripted, Jerry Denton's words at Clark Air Base were not.

The service ended, but the ceremony had only begun. Eight pallbearers carried the casket to a waiting caisson drawn by white mules. A band, resplendent in white navy uniforms, played hymns as the caisson and mules bore Jerry Denton's casket into the deep green of Arlington. More than fifty sailors in white dress marched before and behind Admiral Denton's casket. It was a beautiful pageant to watch.

I stood alongside the surviving members of the Alcatraz Gang as they watched the US Navy bury another one of their brothers beneath Arlington's shady oaks; Ron Storz lay nearby. Seven riflemen cracked the silence with three shots each, a twenty-one-gun salute. A military jet roared high overhead, paying tribute to a rare leader who showed others how to do their duty, be an example, and never surrender faith, hope, or love.

BIBLIOGRAPHY

Alvarez, Everett, Jr., and Anthony S. Pitch. *Chained Eagle: The Heroic Story of the First American Shot Down over North Vietnam.* Washington, DC: Potomac Books, 2005.

Associated Press. "Hanoi Claims Photo Shows Downed Fliers." July 23, 1965.

———. "U.S. Planes Raid North Vietnam." *New York Times,* November 21, 1970: 1, 11.

———. "POW Return Near." *Victoria Advocate,* February 5, 1973: 1.

Atta, Dale Van. *With Honor: Melvin Laird in War, Peace, and Politics.* Madison, WI: University of Wisconsin, 2008.

Austin, Anthony. *The President's War: The Story of the Tonkin Gulf Resolution and How the Nation Was Trapped in Vietnam.* New York: J. B. Lippincott Co., February 1973.

Beech, Keyes. "POWs' Welcome Simple, Heartfelt." *Chicago Daily News Service,* February 1973.

Bruce, David K. "Violations of 1949 Geneva Convention by Democratic Republic of North Vietnam." *Commander's Digest,* January 16, 1971.

Central Committee of the Vietnamese Communist Party. "Politburo Resolution 194: The Policy regarding American Enemy Pilots Captured in Northern Vietnam." Hanoi, November 20, 1969.

Central Intelligence Agency. *Việt Cộng Policy toward and Exploitation of U.S. Prisoners of War.* Declassified, Saigon: CIA, 1967.

Coffee, Gerald. *Beyond Survival: Building on the Hard Times—a POW's Inspiring Story.* New York: Berkley, 1990.

Comptroller, Secretary of Defense. "Casualty Statistics on Southeast Asia, by Month." http://www.americanwarlibrary.com/vietnam/vwc24.htm (accessed August 21, 2012).

Cronkite, Walter. "We Are Mired in a Stalemate" broadcast, February 27, 1968. https://facultystaff.richmond.edu/~ebolt/history398/cronkite_1968.html (accessed February 20, 2018).

Dalton, Anne Chancey. *Jeremiah A. Denton, Jr.: Vietnam War Hero*. Birmingham, AL: Seacoast, 2012.

Davis, Vernon E. *The Long Road Home: U.S. Prisoner of War Policy and Planning in Southeast Asia*. Washington, DC: Historical Office of the Secretary of Defense, 2000.

Defense Prisoner of War/Missing Personnel Office (DPMO). *Personnel Missing, Southeast Asia (PMSEA)*. Washington, DC: Department of Defense, 2005.

Denton, Jeremiah A. *When Hell Was in Session*. Los Angeles: WND Books, 1998.

Denton, Jeremiah A., Jr. Letter to Jane Denton from Hỏa Lò Prison, Hanoi, North Vietnam, December 20, 1965.

Denton, Jeremiah A., III. Interview with Alvin Townley. Virginia Beach, VA. (September 23, 2017).

Department of the Air Force. *Places and Dates of Confinement: Air Force, Navy and Marine Corps POWs, North Vietnam, 1964–1973*. SEAsia PW Analysis Program Report, Washington, DC: Department of the Air Force, 1975.

Department of the Navy. *American War and Military Operations Casualties: Lists and Statistics*. https://www.history.navy.mil/research/library/online-reading-room /title-list-alphabetically/a/american-war-and-military-operations-casualties .html#t7 (accessed June 9, 2018).

Destatte, Robert. Interview with Alvin Townley. Temecula, CA (March 5, 2012).

Foster, Gary. Interview with Alvin Townley. Phone interview (June 28, 2012).

Foster, Gary, and Michael McGrath. *The Hanoi March, July 6, 1966*. Mac's Facts. Colorado Springs, CO: NAMPOW.

Fuller, Byron, with Mike McGrath and Paul Galanti. *Incredible Room 7*. November 17, 2001. http://www.nampows.org/room_7.html (accessed March 1, 2012).

Gallup, George H. *The Gallup Poll: Public Opinion 1935–1971*. http://www .digitalhistory.uh.edu/active_learning/explorations/vietnam/vietnam _pubopinion.cfm (accessed June 9, 2018).

Grubb, Evelyn, and Carol Jose. *You Are Not Forgotten: A Family's Quest for Truth and the Founding of the National League of Families*. St. Petersburg, FL: Vandamere Press, 2008.

Guarino, Larry. *A P.O.W.'s Story: 2801 Days in Hanoi*. New York: Ivy Books, 1990.

Hiên, Nguyby Bern. *Hiên, Prison Historic Vestige*. Hanoi: The Sun Advertising & Trading Co., Ltd., 2010.

Hirsch, James S. *Two Souls Indivisible: The Friendship That Saved Two POWs in Vietnam*. Houghton Mifflin Company: New York, 2004.

Howes, Craig. *Voices of the Vietnam POWs: Witnesses to Their Fight*. New York: Oxford University Press, 1993.

Hubbell, John G. *P.O.W.: A Definitive History of the American Prisoner-of-War Experience in Vietnam, 1964–1973*. New York: Reader's Digest Press, 1976.

International Committee of the Red Cross. Convention (III) relative to the Treatment of Prisoners of War. Geneva, 12 August 1949. https://ihl-databases.icrc.org /applic/ihl/ihl.nsf/States.xsp?xp_viewStates=XPages_NORMStatesParties&xp _treatySelected=375 (accessed April 25, 2018).

Jeremiah (film). Directed by Mark Fastoso, 2016.

Johnson, Lyndon B. "President Johnson's Television Report following Renewed Aggression in the Gulf of Tonkin." University of Texas, School of Information. August 4, 1964. http://solstice.ischool.utexas.edu/projects/index.php/LBJ _Gulf_of_Tonkin_Speech (accessed June 5, 2012).

———. "Report on the Gulf of Tonkin Incident (August 4, 1964)." University of Virginia, Miller Center. https://millercenter.org/the-presidency/presidential-speeches/august-4-1964-report-gulf-tonkin-incident (accessed June 9, 2018).

———. "Speech at Johns Hopkins University: Peace without Conquest (April 7, 1965)." https://millercenter.org/the-presidency/presidential-speeches/april-7 -1965-address-johns-hopkins-university (accessed June 9, 2018).

———. "President Lyndon B. Johnson's Address to the Nation (March 31, 1968)." University of Texas. http://www.lbjlibrary.net/collections/selected-speeches /1968-january-1969/03-31-1968.html (accessed February 25, 2018).

Johnson, Sam, and Jan Winebrenner. *Captive Warriors: A Vietnam POW's Story*. College Station, TX: Texas A&M University Press, 1992.

Karnow, Stanley. *Vietnam: A History*. New York: Penguin, 1983.

Kiley, Frederick, and Stuart I. Rochester. *Honor Bound: American Prisoners of War in Southeast Asia*. Annapolis, MD: Naval Institute Press, 1999.

King, Martin Luther, Jr. "Beyond Vietnam." Address delivered to the Clergy and Laymen Concerned about Vietnam, at Riverside Church, New York City, April 4, 1967.

Laird, Melvin R. "Statement by Secretary of Defense Melvin R. Laird." Washington, DC: Office of Assistant Secretary of Defense (Public Affairs), May 19, 1969.

McCain, John, with Mark Salter. *Faith of My Fathers: A Family Memoir*. New York: Perennial, 1999.

McDaniel, Eugene B. *Scars and Stripes: The True Story of One Man's Courage in Facing Death as a Vietnam POW*. Alexandria, VA: American Defense Institute, 1981.

McGrath, Michael. *Mac's Facts 01—The Big Rooms—Camp Unity*. Colorado Springs, CO: NAMPOW, 2012.

———. *U.S. POWs in North Vietnam*. Colorado Springs, CO: NAMPOW, 2013.

McNamara, Robert S. *In Retrospect: The Tragedy and Lessons of Vietnam*. New York: Random House, 1995.

Mulligan, James A., Jr. *The Hanoi Commitment*. Virginia Beach, VA: RIF Marketing, 1981.

National Archives, Records of the Central Intelligence Agency (263.2589). *CDR Jeremiah A. Denton, Jr.—Report from Inside a Hanoi Prison, 1966*. Hanoi, May 2, 1966.

National Museum of the U.S. Air Force. *Rescue Attempt: The Son Tay Raid*. May 22, 2015. http://www.nationalmuseum.af.mil/Visit/Museum-Exhibits/Fact-Sheets /Display/Article/196019/rescue-attempt-the-son-tay-raid/ (accessed June 9, 2018).

Newsweek. "Home at Last!" February 26, 1973: 16–24.

———. Nixon's "Peace with Honor" broadcast on Vietnam, January 23, 1973. http://watergate.info/1973/01/23/nixon-peace-with-honor-broadcast.html (accessed April 24, 2018).

Nguyen, Lien-Hang T. *Hanoi's War: An International History of the War for Peace in Vietnam*. Chapel Hill, NC: University of North Carolina Press, 2012.

Pepper, Thomas. "1st POWs Leave Hanoi on US Plane." *Sun*, February 12, 1973: A1.

Phóng Viên. "American Air Power under the Eyes of the Victorious People of Hanoi." *People's Army Newspaper*, Issue 1874, July 7, 1966: 1, 4. Translated by Robert J. Destatte, July 6, 2009.

———. "The Streets of the Capital Overflow with Victorious Zeal, Resound with Shouts of Hatred for the American Aggressors." *Hanoi Capital*, July 7, 1966: 1, 3.

Powers, Francis Gary, and Curt Gentry. *Operation Overflight: A Memoir of the U-2 Incident*. Washington, DC: Potomac Books, 2004.

Prisoners of Hope (film). Directed by Bernie Hargis, 2001.

Return with Honor (film). Directed by Freida Lee Mock and Terry Sanders, 1998.

Reuters. "Pilot Captured by Hanoi Supports U.S. Policy." *Saturday Evening Post*, May 8, 1966.

Risner, Robinson C. *The Passing of the Night: My Seven Years as a Prisoner of the North Vietnamese*. Old Saybrook, CT: Konecky & Konecky, 1973.

Rochester, Stuart I. *The Battle Behind Bars: Navy and Marine POWs in the Vietnam War*. Washington Navy Yard, DC: Naval History and Heritage Command and Naval Historical Foundation, 2010.

Rubel, Robert C. "The U.S. Navy's Transition to Jets." *Naval War College Review*, Spring 2010: 49–59.

Rutledge, Howard and Phyllis. *In the Presence of Mine Enemies*. Old Tappen, NJ: Spire Books, 1973.

Schemmer, Benjamin F. *The Raid: The Son Tay Prison Rescue Mission*. New York: Avon, 1976.

Shaffer, Ron. "Admiral Denton Decorated: ExPOW Used His Eyelids to Signal 'Torture.'" *Washington Post*, November 20, 1974: C1.

Stockdale, Jim and Sybil. *In Love and War: The Story of a Family's Ordeal and Sacrifice during the Vietnam Years*. New York: Bantam Books, 1984.

Time. "The War: Hanoi's Pavlovicms." April 14, 1967: 43.

———. "POWs Come Home." February 26, 1973: 13–20.

U.S. House of Representatives. "Hearing on Servicemen Captured and Missing in Southeast Asia." Washington, DC: Library of Congress, April 29, 1970.

Willbanks, James H. "Shock and Awe of Tet Offensive Shattered U.S. Illusions." *U.S. News and World Report*, January 29, 2009.

Wolfe, Tom. *The Right Stuff.* New York: Farrar, Straus & Giroux, 1979.

Young, Stephen. "How Hanoi Won the War." *Wall Street Journal*, August 3, 1995.

Much of the background information for *Captured*, as well as some specifics, came from generous first-person interviews granted by former prisoners of war and their family members. Interviews with the following individuals proved of particular value in this writing:

Commander George Coker, Mrs. Pam Coker, Mr. James Denton, Rear Admiral Jeremiah Denton Jr., Mr. Jeremiah Denton III, Mr. Michael Denton, Colonel Sam Johnson, Mrs. Monica Storz Lovell, Captain Eugene "Red" McDaniel, Captain Michael McGrath, Colonel George McKnight, Captain James Mulligan Jr., Mrs. Louise Mulligan, Rear Admiral Robert Shumaker, Mrs. Janie Tschudy, Commander William Tschudy.

Unless otherwise noted, detailed figures and statistics about POWs are taken from data compiled by Captain J. Michael McGrath, NAMPOW historian.

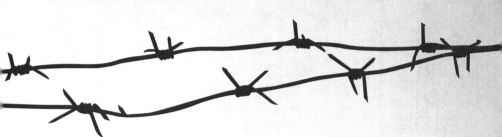

ENDNOTES

"Invictus." Henley, William Ernest. The Poetry Foundation, http://www.poetryfoundation.org/poems/51642/invictus (accessed May 15, 2018).

CHAPTER 1: CAPTURE

"Many flight instructors . . . ejection." Wolfe, *The Right Stuff*, 22. The dawn of the jet age proved costly for pilots, and deaths rose dramatically during the 1950s and 1960s as aircraft became faster and more dangerous.

"By the end . . . and South Vietnam." McNamara, *In Retrospect*, 196.

"Rainbow flight . . . rolling in." Denton, *When Hell Was in Session*, 4.

"Nurture your mind . . . great thoughts." Ibid., 14.

CHAPTER 2: HỎA LÒ PRISON

"He pointed . . . hands and knees." Dalton, *Jeremiah A. Denton, Jr.*, 66.

"The agreement outlined . . . signed the treaty." International Committee of the Red Cross, Convention (III).

"Article I . . . United States of America." Rochester, *The Battle Behind Bars*, 22.

"They asked Jerry . . . were you flying?" Denton, *When Hell Was in Session*, 29. The North Vietnamese had access to American news sources, including armed forces newspapers; they likely learned much of this information on their own but chose, it seems, to continue asking the questions.

"The interrogators grew as weary . . . Geneva Conventions?" Ibid., 30. Owl and Eagle seemed to have been reassigned after the summer of 1965. However, POWs had difficulty knowing to which guard or officer nicknames applied as POWs could describe their captors only via taps and whispers, without visual confirmation. It is clear Jerry Denton did not see either again.

"Shortly, Jerry heard . . . hack 'er." Guarino, *A P.O.W.'s Story*, 35.

"Soon, Guarino . . . being rude." Ibid., 37.

"Go fishing . . . in the latrine." Denton, *When Hell Was in Session*, 41. Additional confirmation obtained via interviews with RADM Robert H. Shumaker, widely considered the most clever and intelligent communicator in Hanoi.

"From his bunk . . . laugh from Guarino." Hubbell, *P.O.W.*, 65.

"Let's take off . . . use it!" Dalton, *Jeremiah A. Denton, Jr.*, 31–33.

"Follow the Code . . . map of the camp." Hubbell, *P.O.W.*, 63.

"Follow the Code . . . antagonize the guards." Guarino, *A P.O.W.'s Story*, 59.

CHAPTER 3: THE ZOO

"All US aggressors . . . humane treatment." Guarino, *A P.O.W.'s Story*, 63–64.

"A twig splintered . . . lock his door." Denton, *When Hell Was in Session*, 52–53.

"Before guards . . . steeled his faith." Ibid., 192.

"A delegation of . . . eat shit!" Hubbell, *P.O.W.*, 142.

"The next morning . . . as well as you have." Ibid.

"During one exchange . . . seven children." Denton, *When Hell Was in Session*, 63. *Jeremiah*, 2016.

"My dearest wife . . . who have given so much for us." Denton, Letter to Jane Denton.

"He visualized . . . return to reality." Denton, *When Hell Was in Session*, 71.

"One day . . . cell shakedown." Hirsch, *Two Souls Indivisible*, 71.

"Mostly, the information . . . same old stuff." Denton, *When Hell Was in Session*, 75.

"When Jerry arrived . . . change your attitude." Ibid., 77–78.

CHAPTER 4: PIGEYE

"But I tell you . . . months alone?" Denton, *When Hell Was in Session*, 84–85.

"Jerry aimed . . . remarry." Hubbell, *P.O.W.*, 172.

CHAPTER 5: THE INTERVIEW

"Desperately he . . . went black." *Prisoners of Hope*, 2001.

"Hey . . . only human," Denton, *When Hell Was in Session*, 87–88.

"He described . . . sickened him." *Time*, "The War: Hanoi's Pavlovicms." Cuban broadcasters who aired the confession reported the voice as that of Jeremiah Denton, but no definitive confirmation was issued.

"He confessed . . . what he has done." Powers and Gentry. *Operation Overflight,* 155.

"Isn't it too . . . say something?" Hubbell, *P.O.W.*, 176. These thoughts must have been in the forefront of Jerry Denton's mind during his interview, and apparently motivated his responses.

"How are you . . . as long as I live." National Archives, *Report from Inside a Hanoi Prison, 1966.* Reuters, "Pilot Captured by Hanoi Supports U.S. Policy."

CHAPTER 6: PARADE

"The announcement . . . will you go?" Hubbell, *P.O.W.*, 201. Mulligan, *The Hanoi Commitment*, 73.

"The Camp Authority . . . defeat their aims." Denton, *When Hell Was in Session*, 107.

"Beyond that . . . harmless and ludicrous." Kiley and Rochester, *Honor Bound*, 164.

"When a confession . . . say what I did." Hubbell, *P.O.W.*, 207.

"Attention, all criminals . . . disgrace." Denton, *When Hell Was in Session*, 109.

"Using toothpaste . . . your leadership." Ibid.

"The POWs never . . . shouted for silence." Hirsch, *Two Souls Indivisible*, 136. Hubbell, *P.O.W.*, 187. Kiley and Rochester, *Honor Bound*, 195. Bob Purcell's sarcastic comment ("I love a parade.") became one of the most widely remembered moments among POWs of the Hanoi March.

"You must remember . . . do with you." Coffee, *Beyond Survival*, 161. Hubbell, *P.O.W.*, 186.

"As the guards prodded . . . heads up!" Denton, *When Hell Was in Session*, 111. Hirsch, *Two Souls Indivisible*, 136–137. Hubbell, *P.O.W.*, 186–187. Numerous POWs recalled Denton's command ("You are Americans! Keep your heads up!") ringing out over the din coming from spectators and guards. POWs did their conscious best not to bow as ordered by the North Vietnamese guards.

"Down with . . . America get out!" Phóng Viên, "American Air Power," 4. The article by an anonymous North Vietnamese journalist (*phóng viên* means "reporter") provides a uniquely North Vietnamese perspective on the events of July 6, 1966.

"One man mocked . . . American air power!'" Ibid., 1.

"He's not going to . . . kill him." Denton, *When Hell Was in Session*, 112. Hubbel, *P.O.W.*, 189.

"As he continued . . . Who had she lost?" *Coffee, Beyond Survival*, 164.

CHAPTER 7: BACK TO THE ZOO

"You fools . . . the people." Denton, *When Hell Was in Session*, 114. Kiley and Rochester, *Honor Bound*, 199.

"Jerry recalled . . . would have won." Denton, *When Hell Was in Session*, 118.

"God, You've got . . . in Your hands." *Jeremiah*, 2016.

"Hi, Jerry . . . God bless you." Mulligan, *The Hanoi Commitment*, 143–144.

"The names . . . collective nickname." Stockdale, *In Love and War*, 241.

CHAPTER 8: LITTLE VEGAS

"In order to atone . . . must be ours." King, "Beyond Vietnam."

"Bow . . . self-interest." Stockdale, *In Love and War*, 252.

"A place . . . war is over." Ibid., 253–254.

"Jerry bowed . . . bad arm." Mulligan, *The Hanoi Commitment*, 159.

"Happy to . . . the window." Denton, *When Hell Was in Session*, 143.

"On August 8 . . . be that long." Hubbell, *P.O.W.*, 300. Mulligan, *The Hanoi Commitment*, 162–163.

"Finally, Jerry said . . . wet down here." Mulligan, *The Hanoi Commitment*, 162–163.

"Jerry arrived . . . Denton alone." Denton, interview with Alvin Townley.

"After pumping Jerry . . . worse was coming." Denton, *When Hell Was in Session*, 147. Hubbell, *P.O.W.*, 360.

CHAPTER 9: ALCATRAZ

"Jerry heard a voice . . . Jerry said." Denton, *When Hell Was in Session*, 149.

"Occasionally, he'd even relive . . . life together." Dalton, *Jeremiah A. Denton, Jr.*, 39–44.

"Dejected, Jerry . . . with his sanity." Kiley and Rochester, *Honor Bound*, 411.

"In Thy gentle . . . smiling our thanks." Rutledge, *In the Presence of Mine Enemies*, 69.

"Sometimes, Jerry's . . . very long message." Denton, *When Hell Was in Session*, 160.

CHAPTER 10: 1968

"He poked . . . like for Christmas?" Denton, *When Hell Was in Session*, 160.

"Howie Rutledge's . . . ticket to Saigon." Ibid.

"Why do you want . . . from your home." Johnson and Winebrenner, *Captive Warriors*, 169.

"Your country has deserted . . . leave us here." Ibid., 169–172.

"To say that we . . . best they could." Cronkite, "We Are Mired in a Stalemate."

"Tonight, I renew . . . your president." President Lyndon B. Johnson's "Address to the Nation."

"Jerry realized . . . will study." Denton, *When Hell Was in Session*, 170–171.

"Mulligan reported . . . won't eat." Mulligan, *The Hanoi Commitment*, 184–185.

"One morning . . . Jerry's body." Denton, *When Hell Was in Session*, 176.

"Knowing the POWs . . . *ordered* you to do it." Denton, *When Hell Was in Session*, 176–177. Denton, interview with Alvin Townley. POWs have noted this moment as an example of Denton's willingness to risk his safety and assume blame to ensure his men's survival.

"Just as Jerry . . . meant it." Denton, *When Hell Was in Session*, 177–179.

"The commandant . . . an order!" Ibid., 180.

CHAPTER 11: CHANGE

"He coached . . . that guy?" Denton, interview with Alvin Townley.

"You were a fool . . . camp radio." Denton, *When Hell Was in Session*, 181.

"He elaborated . . . long as you can." Johnson and Winebrenner, *Captive Warriors*, 177–178.

"You tortured . . . same way." Mulligan, *The Hanoi Commitment*, 195.

"Jerry looked . . . Christmases." Denton, *When Hell Was in Session*, 186.

"He stopped . . . here forever." Denton, Johnson, and Mulligan give different dates and accounts of Ron Storz's collapse; the narrative incorporates the most plausible information from all accounts to portray the most likely time frame and scenario.

"Jerry demanded . . . Brooklyn Bridge." Denton, *When Hell Was in Session*, 194.

"In September 1969 . . . panned Shumaker." Johnson and Winebrenner, *Captive Warriors*, 189.

"That fall . . . not be punish." Denton, *When Hell Was in Session*, 195.

"Jerry understood . . . understand that?" Ibid., 197.

CHAPTER 12: CAMP UNITY

"You bastards . . . going home!" Mulligan, *The Hanoi Commitment*, 211.

"He encountered . . . understand each other." Denton, *When Hell Was in Session*, 202.

"He complained . . . treated well." Johnson and Winebrenner, *Captive Warriors*, 220.

"Eat, Denton . . . and turkey." Mulligan, *The Hanoi Commitment*, 214–215.

"In wrapped . . . drink mix." Ibid., 214.

"There stood . . . each man." *Return with Honor*, 2004.

"Talk eventually . . . Christmas 1970." Johnson and Winebrenner, *Captive Warriors*, 245–246.

"Worship began . . . Americans relent." Accounts of the Church Riot of 1971 vary in their details. The narrative draws on multiple sources, including writings and interviews from participants Jeremiah Denton, Jim Stockdale, Robbie Risner, Howie Rutledge, George Coker, Sam Johnson, and Bob Shumaker. Secondary sources such as Kiley, Rochester, and Hubbell were also consulted in developing the final narrative.

"Jerry considered . . . these allies." Kiley and Rochester, *Honor Bound*, 535–536.

"Troop levels . . . late 1972." Comptroller, Secretary of Defense, "Casualty Statistics."

CHAPTER 13: HOMECOMING

"On January 27 . . . dis . . . *missed*!" Kiley and Rochester, *Honor Bound*, 572. Coffee, *Beyond Survival*, 269–270.

"Then back . . . cautious optimism." Coffee, *Beyond Survival*, 271.

"I haven't answered . . . you're a good man." Denton, *When Hell Was in Session*, 237–238.

"Camp Unity bustled . . . the POWs." Kiley and Rochester, *Honor Bound*, 574. Beech, "POWs' Welcome."

"We are honored . . . God bless America." Denton, *When Hell Was in Session*, 240. *Return with Honor*, 2004. *Jeremiah*, 2016.

PHOTOGRAPH AND MAP CREDITS

JACKET

Jacket photos ©: cover: Naval History and Heritage Command; back cover: Courtesy of DPMO.

BOOK

INDEX

Note: Page numbers in *italics* refer to illustrations.

228

230

232

ACKNOWLEDGMENTS

The captive aviators in Hanoi who endured years of uncertainty and hardship during the Vietnam era deserve the first and last acknowledgment here. They set an unsurpassed example of duty, honor, and perseverance. And to a one, they would say the real heroes were the men fighting it out below the DMZ in South Vietnam.

These former POWs generously shared their stories and perspectives with me and I am grateful. A special circle of these men has become a family to me; I count myself lucky. Special thanks go to the Alcatraz Gang and their family members and particularly to the entire Denton family. They have all been extraordinarily supportive, accommodating, and caring throughout my journey.

In New York, Russ Galen continued to steer me right, and Scholastic's Lisa Sandell helped me ease into a new genre. She embraced this story from the outset and pushed me to tell it better with each edit. Amla Sanghvi proved patient and thorough.

In Atlanta, the Woodruff Arts Center and the Home Depot Foundation have continued to support me and allow me to share the important stories of our POWs and other veterans. Mark Fastoso and the *Jeremiah* team helped inspire me to revisit Jerry Denton's story. My family remains the greatest cheering section for which a writer could hope. And I couldn't have written this without my loving and ever-understanding wife, Suzanne. Writing it would have had less purpose without my daughter, Kensington. I hope this story will resound through generations to inspire her and others after her.

Finally, to the 4th Allied POW Wing, to the Alcatraz Gang, and to the Denton family, GBU.

ABOUT THE AUTHOR

Bestselling author Alvin Townley has traveled the world to discover inspiring stories of leadership, adventure, and purpose. He has written the nationally acclaimed adult books *Legacy of Honor*, *Spirit of Adventure*, *Fly Navy*, and *Defiant* and was part of the Emmy Award–winning team behind the documentary film *Jeremiah*. *Defiant*, which told the story of the leading American prisoners of war in North Vietnam, was called "gripping" by *The New York Times*, "unforgettable" by former president Jimmy Carter, and "riveting" by Senator John McCain. Alvin speaks often, to both youths and adults, about subjects he holds dear, including veterans, character, perseverance, and citizenship. You can learn more at www.AlvinTownley.com and follow him @AlvinTownley.